809.7
F624t

BETHANY
COLLEGE
DISCARDED

# A THEORY OF
# WIT AND HUMOUR

# A THEORY

OF

# WIT AND HUMOUR

BY

F R FLEET

KENNIKAT PRESS
Port Washington, N. Y./London

A THEORY OF WIT AND HUMOUR

First published in 1890
Reissued in 1970 by Kennikat Press
Library of Congress Catalog Card No: 71-105785
ISBN 0-8046-0951-9

Manufactured by Taylor Publishing Company     Dallas, Texas

# CONTENTS.

| CHAP. | | PAGE. |
|---|---|---|
| I. | Introductory | 1 |
| II. | Synopsis of Book ; Definition of Risible Matter; &c. | 6 |
| III. | Classification of Risible Phases | 18 |
| IV. | Moral Perfection (Degrees of) : Injustices | 23 |
| V. | On Ingenuity in General, and "Circumstantial Novelty" | 35 |
| VI. | In Three Parts. Illustration of Phases of Circumstantial Novelty, No. 2 | 59 |
| VII. | Illustration of Phases of Circumstantial Novelty, No. 1 | 162 |
| VIII. | General Illustration of Risible Phases: Class I. | 179 |
| IX. | General Illustration of Risible Phases: Class II. | 206 |
| X. | General Illustration of Risible Phases: Class III. | 238 |
| XI. | Satire, Irony, and Sarcasm | 249 |
| XII. | Miscellaneous | 262 |

# PREFACE.

In producing this work, a few remarks may be made by the author in indication of certain prominent features in which it differs from previous works written by him in the endeavour to analyse wit and humour, the first of which was produced some eight years ago, in a book entitled "An Essay on Wit and Humour, with other Articles." These have been four in number, of which the first three can be said to have no more than a tentative aspect, and need no further mention. The book immediately preceding the present one, and entitled "An Analysis of Wit and Humour," was published in 1888, and, although subsequent revision has revealed not a few inaccuracies in it, the analysis is, the author thinks, substantially correct. At the same time it must be admitted that from some obscurity which in places characterised the book, partly perhaps from difficulty of the subject, but to some extent doubtless from avoidable obscurity of style, the book as a whole certainly lacked attractiveness for the reader.

The book, however, consists, as far as scientific analysis is concerned, exclusively of a theory of risible phases; the other branch of the subject, viz., ingenuity, having merely been treated briefly and generally in a few pages, in ignorance of the circumstance that this, too, admitted of reduction to a science. And thus, although the author is so far of his former opinion as to consider that the publication of 1888 presents the primary substance of a theory of wit and humour, the present work, giving as it does, in Chapters V. and VI., a separate science of ingenuity, is an entirely new production as regards one of the two main divisions of the book; while the other division—the science of risible phases—is a presentation of virtually the whole of the previous book in a largely revised and amended form; though, at the same time, as before stated, the whole essential character of the theory of risible phases remains unaltered.

## CHAPTER I.

INTRODUCTORY.

The precise nature of wit and humour, or of one or other of the two qualities by itself, is a subject towards the apprehension of which it may be said no step has yet been made, though it has occupied the attention of inquirers from time to time, chiefly of late years in the more complete sense of a consideration of the two qualities in connection with—or contradistinction from—each other. Clearly as we may distinguish in their individual aspect most forms of wit and humour, there has been a seemingly insurmountable difficulty in obtaining a starting-point for the construction of a science. There are some who consider the matter hopeless of elucidation, and the average individual, gaily announcing his intention of entering upon the inquiry, is met with a chorus of voices, wrathful, pitying, derisive, or contemptuous, in dissuasion of his venture.

The best known definition of wit, perhaps, is Locke's:—"It lies most in the assemblage of ideas, and putting these together with quickness and variety, wherein can be found any resemblance or congruity, thereby to make up pleasant pictures and agreeable visions to the fancy." Of this, Addison says, "Every resemblance of ideas is not that which we call wit, unless it be such that gives delight and surprise to the reader. These two properties seem essential to wit, more particularly the last of them. In order, therefore, that the resemblance of ideas be wit, it is necessary that the ideas should not lie too near to one another in the nature of things, for where the likeness is obvious it gives no surprise."

It is not clear whether Locke used the word wit in the sense in which we do, and in which Addison evidently understood it, viz., as a quality which in many of its forms produces risibility, some persons, indeed, holding risibility to be a *sine quâ non* of wit, Addison being one of these if we accept surprise as a risible phase. Locke may have confined the term wit to those very ideas to which Addison denies the name, viz., metaphors and non-risible similes, and would then have given some such designation as jocularity or jesting to the risible ingenuities, such as puns,

## INTRODUCTORY.

verbal quibbles, and exaggerated similes. Certainly the words "pleasant pictures and agreeable visions to the fancy" seem to point to an exclusion of anything risible; while Addison's condition of wit, that the ideas should not lie too near to each other in the nature of things, points to the exclusion of everything which is non-risible, thus making his words a total destruction of Locke's definition instead of an amendment of it. The theory presented in this book analyses the several forms of wit in whatever sense the word be used, but in anticipation of the explanations furnished in my theory, I may here mention an ambiguity in one of Locke's words, the non-recognition of which would necessarily be a fundamental source of confusion, and explains how Addison's definition, apparently more or less in accordance with Locke's, is really a total destruction of it. It is this, that the word "congruity," apparently used by Locke in the sense of perfect propriety of connection between the witty idea and its associated phase, has, in its application to ingenious ideas, that meaning, but another as well, viz., a sensible, *i.e.*, an intelligible, connection with the concomitant phase, but at the same time a connection wanting in perfect propriety, which feature it is that produces the surprise required by Addison. Hence Addison contemplating only ideas which are congruous in a partial sense, and Locke only those which are congruous in every way, the two definitions are exclusive of each other.

Of inquiries into the nature of humour, I know of none before the present century. Previous to then, more especially, we may say, in the times of Dryden and Pope, humour was used less as a subject for philosophical speculation than as a weapon of literary warfare. A rough estimate of its general value for offensive purposes, anxiety as to whether by a well-directed cast some individual item of humour would stick; in these directions would lie the main connection with humour of not a few writers of those days. Haylitt and Sydney Smith have treated wit and humour very much after one fashion. Each has discussed a great variety of amusing incidents, but has drawn no line of demarcation between the two qualities. George Eliot has given a general description of them, but not a strict definition. Coleridge, in his *Literary Remains*, gives a definition of humour of a certain originality, but it is of a decidedly exclusive character, and he does not very clearly show its application to the concrete instances be quotes. Mr. H. D. Traill, in the *Fortnightly Review* for September, 1882, defines humour, as no doubt not a few other persons might, as incongruity, though it might be observed that under this definition there can be no humour but what is composed of two phases. The Rev. H. R. Haweis, taking a metaphor from meteorology, calls humour the electric atmosphere and wit the flash. Thackeray has described humour as love and wit, and a not very dissimilar conclusion is that which makes the element of pathos an indispensable condition.

## CHAPTER II.

### SYNOPSIS OF BOOK, AND DEFINITION OF RISIBLE MATTER.

In describing this book as a work on wit and humour, I have employed the words in the common acceptation and in their most comprehensive sense; using the term wit to describe all those ideas to which the word may with any propriety be applied, including what is known as bad and indifferent wit, and humour as applying to all risible ideas whatsoever, some of which would be universally accepted as humour, some whose title to the name, while more or less valid, is less unquestioned, while the remainder usually pass by such names as ludicrousness, incongruity, grotesqueness, buffoonery. Further, my theory, as will be seen, presents a certain extension of the province of the risible as ordinarily understood.

The title of the book, however—though the

## SYNOPSIS; DEFINITION, &c.

matter is merely one of nomenclature—is, as regards wit, by no means closely indicative of the theory presented, the ingenuity usually recognized as wit not always being given that name under my theory, while on the other hand wit is claimed for acts of perception which are not commonly regarded as wit; the apprehension, for instance, of a pun, by the joker's audience.

The following is a short synopsis of the main characteristics of my analysis. In the first place, the preliminary remark is to be made that distinction is observed between incidents which are compound and those which consist of single phases. Then, as to the more characteristic features of the book, a definition and classification is made of risible phases, generally described by the term imperfection * (not being moral deficiency) in actual or fictitious personalities, and specific illustration given in Chapters VIII., IX., and X. In the next place an explanation is presented (see Chapter V.) of the nature of ingenuity in general (so far as a theory of wit and humour would be concerned with ingenuity), which I divide into three species; ingenuity of the first species being shown in such ideas as metaphors, similes (within the limits of sub-

* It is this imperfection in one form or another which furnishes the risible element in any incident, presenting ingenuity, which excites laughter or the smile of risibility as well as admiration.

stantially rational comparison), practical jokes, those expedients in more or less difficult situations which we call mother wit, and a certain proportion of ideas of a description special to my theory (viz., a proportion of what I call "events of the occasion"); ingenuity of the second species—conscious invention as I otherwise call it—comprising all witting invention of risible phases for exhibition in one's self or fictitious ascription to others, and not having a quality which I call circumstantial novelty of the second description; and ingenuity of the third species being the witting invention of phases, risible or non-risible, possessing this quality of circumstantial novelty No. 2. What I call wit is a sub-species of the third species of ingenuity, and is a term applied to the discovery of those phases of circumstantial novelty No. 2 which have, to use the terminology of my theory, a "special connection" with the "events of the occasion;" by reason of being—to use again my own phraseology —"definitel ypresented" by these "events."

Circumstantial novelty No. 1 is explained and illustrated in detail in Chapter VII.

I may add that an exhibition of moral inferiority is the reverse of what I define as a risible phase, implying, as it does, unless and until punishment is given, some gain to the exhibitor, and a proportionate loss to another or others.

As being, however, procedure which the exhibitor does not as a rule like to be made prominent, it stands on the same footing with a risible phase, so far as regards its being matter for notice (with the introduction of some element of risibility) by another.

In the arrangement of chapters I have not followed the strictly logical order throughout, but that which most quickly shows the entire theory in its essential features. Thus, having given in Chapter III. a general idea of the nature of risible phases, I postpone detailed illustration of these till I have presented the other main branch of my theory, viz., that relating to the three species of ingenuity, and circumstantial novelty No. 2.

For convenience of reference, the several incidents given as illustrations are numbered in a progressive series for each chapter containing illustrations. There are, however, a few forms of imperfection which scarcely require specific incidents, but merely general illustrations to explain them, and these I have left unnumbered.

I would here observe, less for the guidance of the responsible critic than for that of the general reader, that while in some few of my illustrations there are matters which demand some slight or extra tax upon the attention, there is, I think, even without these, a body and variety of illustration sufficient for an apprehension of the precise nature of the theory, and estimate of its correctness, although my illustrations in Chapter VI. certainly fall short in one or two places of what might properly be given. These special demands upon the attention may be due in one or two places not only to intricacy in the subject itself, but to more or less obscurity— it may be dubiousness—in my treatment of it; there being in one instance—my postulate of the quality of moral dignity—what is possibly no other than an arbitrary assumption, though this is not an error—if an error it be — which would cause any confusion in the general theory. I do not know that there are, apart from this lastly-mentioned question, any substantial shortcomings in the three chapters illustrating risible phases in detail, though if there are, that branch of the theory is not one whose characteristic aspect would be affected by occasional details of individual sections. And a claim to general correctness may, I hope, be made for Chapter VI.

To mark off, then, what may be considered the less readable portions of the book, including under this designation not only what is in any way intricate or obscure, but matter which is uninteresting merely, if it is only of minor importance in the theory,—the reader, if so disposed, could omit anything more than a casual inspection of the whole of Chapter IV., after the first page or so ; all the remarks in Chapter V. on Evidence of Ingenuity, except the paragraph and passage following it wherein is pointed out and emphasized a distinction between a phase of circumstantial novelty in a joke and the profession of belief in its accordance with common sense which is often made ; anything in Chapter VI. beyond what will show the general plan, though I scarcely think any appreciable difficulty will be found there ; and in the chapters illustrating risible phases, the whole of Sect. I., Chapter VIII., except the first two pages ; the latter half of Sect. VI., Chapter VIII. ; and the classification forming the latter portion of the discussion of errors of judgment, Sect. I., Chapter IX.

To state now my definition of risible phases : These are those phases of imperfection in beings possessing in reality or in the imagination the capacities for pleasure and pain, which are noticeable—attract the attention of the observer—from their being either only occasional conditions with anyone, or not common to a generality of persons. They are grouped under three general phases, viz. (1) really or apparently involuntary retrogression in respect of welfare by means of loss or pain ; * (2) experience of obstruction of

* The punishments inflicted by law do not come within this category, implying, as they do, previous unlawful gain, and thus effecting not retrogression, but the *status quo ante*.

legitimate progress; and (3) inferiority to certain standards of perfection (not being in respect of morality, inferiority in which direction is the reverse of risible), which standards will be duly particularized. And I would here mention that where the word imperfection is used without prefix, it will signify risible imperfection, and likewise the word inferiority without prefix will signify one of the forms of the third phase of risible imperfection. Where imperfection or inferiority in respect of morality is to be referred to, the prefix of moral will be given.

I use the word perfection, as applied to individuals, as synonymous, except as regards moral perfection, which I shall speak of hereafter—in Chapter IV.—with the utmost condition of pleasure to the individual; the degree of imperfection indicated in any phase exhibited being in proportion to the distance it places the individual from a condition of the utmost pleasure, the phases of pain representing, according to the degree of the pain, extension of such distance beyond the point of a neutral state as regards emotion, thus representing imperfection in degree according to the distance. To a condition of pleasure there is needed not only the possession of property with the potentiality of giving pleasure, but the capacity to enjoy it; and likewise to a

## OF RISIBLE MATTER, &c.

condition of pain is needed possession of property with the potentiality of giving pain, and the capacity to receive pain from it. A person's own abilities or endowments are property only capable in the main of giving him pleasure indirectly, by exchange for the productions of nature and of his fellows. But although abilities or endowments calculated to procure pleasure from nature or man in exchange for their exercise or exhibition need, in order to produce a condition of pleasure, the complement of the property for which they are to be exchanged, they are equivalent to an indication of such condition, since in the ordinary course of events the complemental property follows, the recognition of which circumstance by the observer gives the abilities or endowments all the appearance of indicating the condition of pleasure.

These remarks would be applicable to the lower animals to a substantial degree. Of course, with wild animals the exchange for the exercise of their abilities would be mainly with nature, while the return received from man by domesticated animals for their services or value as food would depend on their owners. To inanimate objects endowed in imagination with life and voluntary action, and to ideal personages such as fairies, elves, and goblins, the remarks would also be substantially applicable.

It is true the witting production of a risible

phase of appreciable value to the intellectual sense implies excellence (the reverse of risible imperfection), whether the risible phase be exhibited in the inventor's own person or fictitiously ascribed to another person, real or imaginary. But this excellence is in another department of procedure than that of the risible phase, the department, namely, of invention of phases thus pleasing the intellectual sense on account of their novelty. In the particular line or direction of procedure to which the risible phase pertains, the imperfection remains in exhibition, though of course where an imperfection is recognized as wittingly exhibited it is not attended by the incidental disadvantages which would follow an unavoidable exhibition of imperfection, such, for instance, as the termination of association with a person which might result from a serious exhibition by the latter of inferior mental or physical abilities.

It is, of course, to incorrect or absurd opinions thus expressed with risibility as the sole object or one of the objects in view, that the word "ostensible," so familiar an expression in connection with risibility, is applied.

Of course, with many of what I have called risible imperfections, the presence of sympathy in the observer, or, failing this, the sense that it is called for, would preclude laughter or the smile of risibility. I have defined the imperfections as risible on the strength of the assumption of their potentiality of exciting in the observer a moral— and egoistic—emotion of pleasure at the alteration of relative status between the parties caused by the imperfection, which potentiality, however, would be outweighed in many cases by the above emotion of sympathy or the sense that it is demanded by the occasion. Whether I am right in assuming in all these imperfections the above potentiality or effect, and their risibility on that account, is open to question, but if, as I hope, I have in my analysis more or less correctly indicated the source of the whole substantial interest we take in, and have properly classified, such phases as are admittedly risible, at least all practical purposes will have been served, and my theory be virtually independent of this other question.

The source of the pleasure taken in admittedly risible phases, or at least in such as are forcible enough to excite laughter in anyone, would seem from the well-known definition of laughter by Hobbes, to be considered by him as being entirely a moral emotion. Laughter, he says, "is a sudden glory arising from some sudden conception of some eminency in ourselves by comparison with the inferiority of others, or with our own formerly." But it would seem clear that the pleasure expressed by laughter is with persons of experience and discrimination only to a very small extent due to a moral emotion at alteration of relative status between the observed and observer, and is mainly an intellectual pleasure. And probably even with the uncultured and inexperienced the pleasure is more intellectual than moral.

Why our pleasure in certain ideas is expressed in the particular outward form of laughter, or the smile of risibility, is of course purely a matter for speculation. Possibly, it seems to me, this mode of expression may be due to a tendency of the mind instinctively to look for progress or absence of retrogression in one's self and others, whereby the reverse of these, as are risible imperfections, may cause a retrograde process in the mind of the observer, the conflict of which process with the opposite tendency natural to the mind may be what gives the expression of pleasure the particular form of laughter or the smile of risibility.

The degrees of novelty in risible phases vary indefinitely, from those too slight to make a risible phase worth producing intentionally—that is, solely for its value to the intellectual sense of the observer—to those of very considerable value to the intellectual sense. And the novelty appears to me to be of two descriptions, the first being intrinsic—a novelty possessed by risible phases at all times, pertaining as it does to the phase in itself; and the second, circumstantial, or extrinsic

—a novelty possessed by risible phases on occasion, according to the circumstances under which they are presented. Risible phases having no circumstantial novelty seldom have much value for persons of discrimination, though presentation or representation of such of them as admit of it, in metre or rhythmical form, will give these an adventitious value. The risible phases possessing circumstantial novelty, as will be shown hereafter, may have any degree of value, according to the occasion. In many cases a risible phase, whether with or without circumstantial novelty, though oftenest without, will be only a part of an incident, and sometimes a merely secondary feature.

Where one's sympathy is excited to any material extent by an imperfection, or—sympathy being absent—the case is recognized as one calling for sympathy, the effect the imperfection would otherwise have would be modified, and at times, as in the commoner forms of retrogression and obstruction, be destroyed. But where the disadvantage resulting from the imperfection is inappreciable, as, for instance, a loss of a few seconds' time, or a slip of the tongue, and with most imperfections occurring in fiction only, there is, of course, propriety in its reception by laughter or a smile.

## CHAPTER III.

### CLASSIFICATION OF RISIBLE PHASES, WITH INCIDENTAL REMARKS.

THE forms in which imperfection in the foregoing three phases—really or apparently involuntary retrogression in respect of welfare, obstruction, and inferiority (not being moral)—is shown, I should divide into three classes. The first class—composed mainly of imperfection in the form of retrogression and obstruction—relates for the most part to property other than the mental and physical possessions of the individual, and has the following sections:—I. Diminution, depreciation in value, or total loss, of valuable property owned, without compensation or return in kind, or in the shape of thanks, or of a feeling of having performed a duty by the proceeding; evidence of absence of esteem commonly supposed to be accorded to the particular individual; or evidence of the possession of an expectation or of a pros-

## CLASSIFICATION OF RISIBLE PHASES.

pect of diminution, depreciation, or loss, of valuable property. II. Possession of property giving pain, or evidence of expectation or of prospect of this, also without compensation in some form. III. Experience of obstruction of legitimate progress. IV. Evidence of absence of ownership of some special property or benefits common to the generality, or evidence of ownership of property of that description, of less extent or of less value than that owned by the generality. V. A less favourable situation than that of the generality in respect of environment or external conditions. VI. Loss of dignity. VII. Appropriation of articles of utility to other than their commonly intended purposes.

The second class (imperfection in the form of inferiority) relates more especially to the personal character, and has the following sections:—
I. Exhibition in transient or in permanent form, that is, by transient or permanent productions, of capabilities, acquirements, or endowments, of an inferior degree; exhibition of the absence of capabilities, acquirements, or endowments, in some direction; and exhibition of absence of any capacity for enjoyment common to the generality. II. Various divergences from conditions familiar to the observer; and various alterations in the existing order of things generally, that is to say, various innovations. III. Inferiority in special

walks of life to the generality engaged in those directions. IV. Inferiority attributed in idea to the Deity; and also to Nature, regarded as a personality. V. Inferiority in inanimate objects.

The third class is that of incongruous juxtaposition, which is also a form of inferiority.

Not only the individual, but all aggregate bodies having common interests may exhibit imperfection, as seen in public obstruction, and deprivation by destruction of public property.

As regards the standard, that is, the superior measure of perfection, to which an inferiority is referable by the observer;—with a large proportion of imperfections the standard is the intellectual condition of the generality, irrespective of class or community (that is, the intellectual condition of the generality in respect of its natural, not acquired, capabilities), or its physical condition. In other cases the inferiority is referable to the measure of culture or education possessed by particular grades of society. In others to the particular customs, manners, or costumes, of nations. In other cases, inferiority, while not referable to a standard of procedure possessed by the generality, is referable to a standard apprehended by it; the proceeding relating to a special art or profession in which the generality are not engaged (it being understood that the matter is

## OF RISIBLE PHASES. 21

not one of technical import, but one of which the unprofessional individual is able to judge in virtue of the possession of ordinary common sense).

The standards to which inferiority attributed in imagination to the Deity and Nature, and to inanimate objects, are referable, will be mentioned as occasion arrives for illustrating these forms of inferiority.

There are two further descriptions of imperfection, in the shape of inferior mental capabilities (Sect. I., Class II.) which are not intrinsic inferiorities, referable to the standard of a generality. The first, which I call an adventitious inferiority, is shown in error of judgment of every kind (in addition to any intrinsic inferiority such error may happen to show) the inferiority—of a fixed and mechanical character—being in reference to everyone in possession, whether by his own acumen or by knowledge otherwise acquired, of the data necessary to have avoided the error. The second (a quite unimportant feature, as being but a small matter of detail) I call an incidental inferiority, and is shown by any person who puts forward with an intention (real, or ostensible only, according as we may think) to deceive, a statement discredited really or professedly by the recipient.

As above implied, a judgment, whether or not events show it to be erroneous, may indicate intrinsic inferiority in the matter of reasoning power, or not, according to its character. Again, when error of judgment entails loss of any kind (beyond the unrecompensed loss of time spent in forming the judgment, which would only be a risible imperfection if the judgment showed intrinsic inferiority) there is in such loss imperfection in a further direction shown.

Humour in fiction may of course be either true to nature, that is, similar in character to occurrences of real life, or not. In the latter cases alike with the former, the imperfection is referable to the standard existing in real life in the phase to which the procedure relates.

## CHAPTER IV.

### ON MORAL PERFECTION, AND INJUSTICE FROM THE MORAL POINT OF VIEW.

In this chapter I state the relation to my thesis of degrees of moral perfection above and below the average, and treat more especially from the moral as distinguished from the risible point of view, so far as is necessary to my thesis, of injustice committed for the sake of jocularity or otherwise. Injustices, except where they are accidental and, further, indicate no culpable negligence, of course imply moral inferiority, real or formal, in the offender, while without exception they involve risible imperfection in the offended party, in the shape either of retrogression or experience of obstruction of legitimate progress.

Before proceeding to these matters I may make a general observation respecting risible imperfections presenting an appreciable moral aspect, whether caused by injustice or not, viz., that the predominance of the moral over the risible aspect, or *vice versâ*, would depend upon various circumstances, such as the probability of an injustice being intended to injure, the respective forces of the two aspects—moral and risible—of the case, the question whether the incident was fictitious or of actual occurrence, and the presence or absence of sympathy in the observer.

Moral excellence differs from the corresponding degree of perfection in respect of personal welfare in that the former is in proportion, or in somewhat close proportion, to the sacrifice made of intellectual, æsthetic, or physical pleasures. With the question as to the precise extent to which there are compensations for these sacrifices in the shape of pleasure in doing good, and with the question of future recompense, my thesis is not concerned. But it is obvious that there is not seldom only a partial recompense visibly accruing for these sacrifices, and on such occasions the sacrifice would be identical in character with risible imperfection in the shape of involuntary retrogression. The voluntary nature of the sacrifice, however, in conjunction of course with the fact that it is more or less rational, would deprive it of all appearance of a risible imperfection; and thus in effect moral excellence in no wise concerns my theory.

To refer now to injustices. Many of these, and the risible imperfections resulting from them, are so plainly definable that nothing need be said of them here. Such are interferences with rights, public or private, in the shape of prevention, by obstruction, of legitimate progress, destruction of valuable property or diminution of its value, and displacement of it; the risible imperfection caused by the latter offence being loss of valuable property in the shape of time and energy spent in seeking or replacing the property. Practical jokes causing risible imperfections in various ways are another common form of interference.

With other injustices the precise direction in which the injustice lies or the risible imperfection resulting from it is not so obvious, and these, therefore, call for some remark.

The offence of, without just cause, applying to a person an epithet, such as scoundrel or villain, indicating general moral inferiority in him, or, likewise unjustly, accusing another of any particular injustice, seriously, in the belief that the charge is just, or jocularly, under the pretence of such belief, causes an exhibition by the accused of risible imperfection (of Sect. I. Class I. of risible phases) by reason of the evidence of diminution, really or ostensibly only, of the esteem which had been supposed (by a person or persons other than the accuser) to be accorded by the accuser to the other on account of moral merit, the counterbalancing gain from real moral inferiority, which would prevent diminution of esteem from involving risible imperfection, being absent here. The exhibition of risible imperfection would be made only to such as believed in or knew of the accused person's innocence of the charge.

Where the charge is seriously made, the diminution of esteem being then of course real, not ostensible only, the moral aspect of the injustice would outweigh to the observer the slight risible element, while when the charge is jocular, the moral aspect being then merely formal, the risible imperfection—the ostensible diminution of esteem—becomes prominent, and claims a smile.

An unjust imputation to a person, made seriously or jocularly, of a lower degree of perfection, other than moral, than he or others thought pertained to him would, as with unjust imputations in regard to moral standing, cause imperfection in the person unjustly depreciated, of Sect. I. Class I.; the exhibition being made only to such as imputed the higher degree of perfection.

Dishonourable conduct—betrayal of trust—is, of course, an injustice; involving necessarily exhibition in another of some form of risible imperfection, made to every person knowing of the procedure and of its character, while the like

## MORAL PERFECTION: INJUSTICES.

exhibition would be made in respect of conduct erroneously regarded as dishonourable by anyone. In addition to its non-risible character of injustice to others, all such conduct, it seems to me, involves a risible imperfection in the defaulter in the shape of a lack of the natural moral dignity of man (Sect. VI. Class I. of risible phases). Dishonourable procedure may be divided into the two categories of (1) actions, with omission to act as demanded by honour, and (2) speeches, or written statements, with which we may group indications of thought other than by language, such indications being of varying degrees of definiteness.

(1) Abstraction of the money of others entrusted to one may be mentioned as one of the commoner forms of dishonourable actions, the loss of the money being of course the risible imperfection caused.

Dishonour is shown in the procedure we call discourtesy or impoliteness—betrayals of trust in a large number of matters which are usually not grave enough and often not sufficiently definite to be dealt with by law. Under the category of dishonourable actions in this direction—of discourtesy, would come offences, no detailed illustrations of which need here be given, of commission, omission, and refusal to comply with applications for the exhibition of courtesy needed by others.

The imperfection caused in another by discourteous actions may take the forms of retrogression, of demonstrable obstruction of legitimate progress, or of obstruction which is not demonstrable. Retrogression is seen where small damages or deterioration of one's clothes are caused by another's carelessness. Demonstrable obstruction of legitimate progress is seen where a person blocks a public thoroughfare. Obstruction which is not demonstrable would be caused when a request to another to do one some small service, costing him little or nothing, is refused. The progress desired is, though not demonstrably, yet presumably legitimate, because the presumption is that the person asking the favour renders an equal quantity of these services to his fellows.

All discourtesy appears to me to involve, in addition to the risible imperfection in the form of lack of moral dignity, which, as I have mentioned, dishonour in general implies, a risible imperfection in the shape of loss of intellectual dignity, by reason of the petty character of the dishonour.

(2) Falsehoods, or intentional misrepresentations of events, may be divided into the three classes of the serious, the jocular, and the nominal; the serious being dishonest or otherwise according to whether the object is a material benefit or some practical joke or other hoax; the jocular being those not expected to be believed in,

## MORAL PERFECTION: INJUSTICES.

and the nominal falsehoods being those not constituting attempts, serious or jocular, at deceit,* among this class being included such imaginative literature and narrations as are not expressly stated to be ideal only, though as regards these latter, perhaps we should say that although it may not be stated in the work itself, or by the narrator, that the statement is fictitious, we may take an intimation to that effect as understood to have been made through another channel, viz., that through which our knowledge of the fictitious character of much literature has reached us.

In any case nominal falsehoods are without any of the appearance of offence which real falsehoods, serious or jocular, have; nor is any risible imperfection on the part of the recipient involved in them.

The risible imperfection necessarily caused in a person to whom a falsehood is told,—imperfection exhibited to such as know of or believe in the falsity of the statement,—would, it seems to me, be obstruction of the progress which the reception

---

* The conditions excluding a false statement from the category of attempts at deceit, would seem to be, assuming the recipient of the falsehood to be an adult, the presence of two or more of the following three conditions: (1) the statement being the profession of an opinion only, the correctness of which may be easily ascertained elsewhere; (2) no material issues being involved in the statement; and (3) the opinion being contrary to common sense, making it unlikely that the recipient would believe in the statement.

of true information affords if acted on, except where the information is of that description whose use would be the redress of injustice, when the necessary effect of the falsehood as regards risibility would be not obstruction of the possibility of progress, but the continuance of the risible imperfection caused by the injustice, instead of its termination by reason of redress being obtained in the shape of punishment or compensation. And in any procedure taken in the belief or hope that a false statement is or may be true there would be further risible imperfection in the shape of loss of time, money, energy, etc., alike where the object was progress and where it was the redress of injustice.

Such conduct as slander involves necessarily diminution of esteem for the slandered person which was previously accorded by those imposed on by the slander. While there may be caused on occasion experience of obstruction of legitimate progress on the part of the slandered person, through social ostracism resulting from the falsehood.

It would seem that where a single falsehood or systematic misrepresentation is in such a direction that there is no reasonable probability that it will be permanently successful—will result in other than a net loss to the producer—we recognize it when exposed as indicating intellectual and thus risible, as well as moral, inferiority. When, for instance, a serious deception has been exercised respecting the procedure of a third person from whom information of his actions could easily be obtained by the person to whom the lie is told, there is intellectual inferiority shown. We should not regard these falsehoods as having been wholly unaccompanied by a prospect of gain to the producer, but they would be so obviously unworthy of the risk of detection as to indicate an intellectual inferiority.

Another form of dishonourable speech is language which we call discourteous on account of its matter; this form of discourtesy being the indication to a person or before his presence, from other motives than the interests of morality, of moral or other inferiority in him to the average individual, convention giving everyone the right to be treated in his presence as possessing average intellectual, æsthetic, and social, qualities, whatever his may really be, and as possessing average morality provided he shows moral inferiority of no graver description than venial offences. This procedure is synonymously described as the communication of unnecessary truths, or supposed truths, of an unpleasant nature.

Of course, if a person refers to this moral inferiority in the interests of morality, we recognize an imperative object before which considerations of courtesy must disappear.

Speech which is discourteous on account of tone or manner is dishonourable, it appears to me, because the generality of members of society trust their fellows to show in their exchange of speech a sense of equality in respect that the information and other services which one obtains by speech with one's fellows are voluntarily afforded by them, and could be withheld if they chose. This recognition of equality is made in the employment of such phrases as : If you please —be good enough—will you, etc., etc. ; or, without the employment of actual words indicating request, in the adoption of what we recognize as a tone of request, not demand. The discourteous person shows no recognition of the equality which exists in this direction between himself and others, but speaks as if he had power to compel the benefits of social intercourse, thus betraying the trust put in him by his fellows to do as they do—make recognition in their words, or tone, of equality in the above respect. The form which the risible imperfection in the person addressed by the discourteous individual takes would be the loss of esteem which a member of society is presumed to accord to his fellows in virtue of their holding this position of equality with him. This imperfection would, of course, be not affected by any preclusion of progress through ostracism which a discourteous person might experience. The very fact of discourteous speech involves loss of esteem, a loss which it needs but like language or tone in return to cause in the other.

Conceit, pride, and vanity may be described as being in some cases indications by word, tone, or manner, of a sense of some superiority to society, or sections of it, which is not generally admitted, and in others, gratuitous, *i.e.*, unnecessary, indications of an admitted superiority. These qualities, in whatever shape they are exhibited, naturally must give offence, but it may, I suppose, be said that they indicate injustice only when shown gratuitously. The injustice, it would seem, is by reason of society considering that justice is observed in the enjoyment by a person possessing any qualities of superiority, of such benefits therefrom as may accrue to him in other ways than unnecessarily reminding society, or a section of it, of its inferiority to him in the qualities in which he excels—the benefits, namely, which may accrue to him in the shape of material advantages, and society's esteem. (The inferiority on the part of society is, of course, not a risible one, being the degree of perfection possessed by the generality, though in the shape of feelings of annoyance or indignation, society would show imperfection, of Sect. II., Class 1.) And since society, as the stronger party, is presumably able to enforce justice in this respect, the injustice would take the form of dishonour, though not the particular form of discourtesy, for the rules of courtesy would not seem to be violated here.

When a person is aware that he is committing injustice in gratuitous exhibition of conceit, etc., the exhibition would not involve mental inferiority, unless, that is, the superiority was not generally admitted. Those, however, who were not aware that the gratuitous evidence of conceit in them was unjust, or not aware that they were showing the quality, would in respect of their ignorance exhibit (along with their unintentional dishonour) risible imperfection in the shape of inferiority (intrinsic) of mental perception. While, of course, all those who claimed a superiority which was not generally considered to exist would be regarded as exhibiting mental inferiority on that account.

## CHAPTER V.

### ON INGENUITY IN GENERAL, AND CIRCUMSTANTIAL NOVELTY.

The ingenuity with which a theory of wit and humour is concerned relates, with a few such exceptions as mother wit and various other ideas of practical value, to phases mainly interesting the intellectual sense of persons in general. As stated in the synopsis in Chapter II., which I recapitulate in various particulars, it comprises three species.

The first, which will be designated throughout the book by the term, ingenuity of the first species, is the discovery, by special search, of various ideas, to be enumerated in detail later on, and of which a general description has been given in the synopsis.

The second species, which may be otherwise designated as conscious invention (a term appropriate because the like phases to those discovered by this species of ingenuity are often produced in unconsciousness of their risible nature), is the discovery, by special search, of risible phases, with or without circumstantial novelty No. 1 (circumstantial novelty from the presence of an excuse for imperfection) for jocular exhibition in one's self, or for ascription to fictitious personages, as in novels, or fictitiously, to existing persons.

It is often convenient (as giving a certain excuse for the joke) when presenting a phase of circumstantial novelty No. 2 opposed to common sense, to profess belief in the full propriety—the conformity with common sense—of such presentation. This profession, when it is an ostensible mental inferiority and not a nominal falsehood,* would be a phase of conscious invention, though of course one of a fixed and uniform character, and wholly without interest in itself.

The third species is the discovery, by special search, of phases, risible or non-risible as the case may be, of circumstantial novelty No. 2 (circumstantial novelty from remoteness of the phase from the ordinary mental range), the discovery of such of these phases as have what I have called a "special connection with the events of the occasion," being a sub-species, for which I reserve the term wit.

There are diverse conditions attending the dis-

* A phase of this latter description being produced by ingenuity of the first species.

covery of phases of circumstantial novelty No. 2, in respect of such several matters as expression of the phase of novelty, presentation without expression, expression with necessity of apprehension by the observer (*i.e.*, appropriation of an utterance exclusively to the expression of the phase of novelty), expression without that necessity: also in respect of the presence or absence of a uniform or formal presumptive evidence of ingenuity. A diversity of condition in this last respect is somewhat rare, the formal presumptive evidence being present in most cases; the few occasions where it is absent being those of incidents where it is either superseded by positive evidence of ingenuity of the third species, or those where, from the phase of novelty being a mental imperfection in the presenter, the evidence of ingenuity of the third species, if there is any, is merely arbitrary. These diversities of condition, and the precise meaning or application of the various terms I have just been using, will be elucidated, explained, and illustrated in this and the following chapter.

Circumstantial novelty—that is, novelty attaching to a phase by reason of a connection with particular circumstances, and giving it an extrinsic value—as I have said, is of two descriptions, of which the following is a general statement.

Novelty of the first description is received on

occasion by certain mental inferiorities by reason of the existence of an excuse for the imperfection. Novelty of the second is received on occasion by phases in general, risible and non-risible (risibility in a phase being only an incidental feature), by reason of the phase having a more or less sensible connection with a phase or phases definitely placed before one, while being more or less remote from the ordinary mental range, with the latter phase or phases in view without the former.

Beyond a particular statement of the conditions giving circumstantial novelty No. 1, nothing is needed by way of explanation of this description of novelty; and the particulars of the conditions will accordingly be incorporated in the same chapter (VII.) which gives the illustrations, being omitted here as too long for convenient repetition.

These phases, it may be observed, are not, like those receiving circumstantial novelty No. 2, almost without exception formally recognizable as due to ingenuity, but in common with risible phases without circumstantial novelty No. 1, are of serious exhibition or are due to ingenuity (conscious invention) according to circumstances.

With regard to circumstantial novelty No. 2, considerable explanation is required on such matters as various general causes of the novelty in various groups of incidents; substantial dif-

## AND CIRCUMSTANTIAL NOVELTY. 39

ferences in the value of the novelty,—a difference in one case, viz., puns, characterising an entire group of incidents, but generally depending upon the nature of the particular incident of a group; elucidation of special phrases; and incidental remarks. These explanations, etc., are given in the present chapter.

Stating now in full the conditions giving circumstantial novelty No. 2, these are—(1) a more or less sensible connection of the phase with some verbal expression (expressions, as regards group No. 4, Chapter VI.) or with some event not verbally indicated, which we may call the event (or, in group No. 4, events) of the occasion; and (2) remoteness* from the range of the mind ordinarily with the event or events of the occasion in view.†

The phases of novelty form two classes. Those of the first have a legitimate connection with the event or events of the occasion, from their being

---

\* Momentarily with everyone, and for a longer time or permanently according to the nature of the phase of novelty or the ability of the particular person or persons concerned.

† In the majority of jokes we have the event of the occasion produced first, and the phase of novelty at a subsequent time put forward by verbal expression. In puns and a few other cases the event of the occasion is produced, and the phase of novelty easily perceived by most persons a moment later, expression being unnecessary on that account. Where there is what I call a concomitant and incidental event of the occasion, it is produced, in relation to the primary event, in varying order according to circumstances.

phases which, according to their particular description, are either in the actual course of things before their discovery;* are reasonably possible of being in the actual course of things before their discovery;† are reasonably possible of realization in the external world;‡ are more or less appropriate—as being of a natural character or otherwise legitimate—of being brought into (immediate) future connection with the event of the occasion;§ or are phases which, while not reasonably possible of realization, are given legitimacy of connection by the laws of hyperbole, or by the license of ridicule.‖ Phases of novelty of the second class have, while a sensible, yet in no wise a legitimate, connection with the event of the occasion.

The term "reasonable possibility of realization" (in the past or future), which with certain phases determines the class to which they belong, is used in the liberal and comprehensive sense which is demanded when, as is usually the case in a theory of this kind, the intellectual as distinguished from the practical aspect of the phase is regarded;

* *e.g.*, the second signification of a pun; the remote particular interpretation of a general utterance the expression of which constitutes a verbal quibble; and illustrations Nos. 1 and 2, Chapter VI., Part II.

† *e.g.*, Nos. 5 to 17, Chapter VI., Part II.

‡ See Nos. 3 and 4, Chapter VI., Part II.

§ See Nos. 18 to 25, Chapter VI., Part II.

‖ See Obvious Exaggerations, Chapter VI., Part III.; and No. 3, Chapter VI., Part III.

the expression applying to all phases whose actuality is not incompatible with the laws of nature. This definition, though not perhaps clearly comprehensible at present, will, I think, become so when taken in connection with the illustrations in the next chapter. At the same time I should observe that it is not a primary essential that any division into classes of phases of circumstantial novelty No. 2 should be made—that any definition of what is reasonably possible of realization should be supplied; the circumstance of a phase of novelty possessing "legitimacy" of connection, not being of further import than that it gives the phase a certain specific element of value.

Of the phases of novelty in class 1, a large proportion have a connection which I may call special, from the phase being, while unperceived for the moment or longer, definitely presented wholly or, as to one group of incidents, in part, by the events of the occasion.* This definite presentation takes place by reason of the phase being either comprised in, while not being expressed by, the events of the occasion (instances of these phases being found in the remote particular interpretations of general utterances constituting the

* The plural word "events" may be conveniently used as a rule to signify indifferently a single event when the occasion presents but one, or two when there are two of them.

ordinary form of verbal quibble, and in identities and antitheses) ; expressed, while not immediately perceptible, if perceived at all, (as with puns); expressed, while not noted, because ignored by convention (these phases being the literal interpretations of metaphors and idioms); expressed as regards one or more of its main features (see Nos. 25 to 32, Chapter VI., Part I.) ; or, while not being thus comprised in or expressed by the events of the occasion, is yet definitely presented by them, from the phase having either what I call an "exceptional immediate connection" with the events of the occasion, or an "invariable immediate class connection" with them.

The exceptional immediate connections form two varieties; in the first—the incidents here relating solely to human procedure—the phase of novelty being of special importance, from being of an undesirable character; and in the second —these incidents relating to external nature— the phase of novelty having a like special importance from its being remarkable. The connections are called exceptional because the events of the description of those in these incidents commonly have no phases of special importance immediately connected with them.

The invariable immediate class connection I have mentioned is that which a phase possesses from belonging to a class of ideas any one of which is—according to which of the two divisions of this group of incidents it belongs to—reasonably possible of actual immediate association in the present with the events of the occasion, or more or less natural or appropriate of actual association in the immediate future with the events.

The rest of the phases of class I. have, from their not being thus definitely presented by the events of the occasion, a general connection only with them ; as have for the same reason all the phases of class II.

The circumstances which I call the "events of the occasion" call for one or two observations.

They are mainly single events, and verbal expressions. To specify them in a few groups ;—in puns the event is a verbal expression, with an easily perceived second signification ; the event of the occasion being the form of words in the first signification, and the remote phase—the phase of circumstantial novelty No. 2—the second signification. With a verbal quibble the event of the occasion is a general utterance, and the remote phase a particular interpretation other than that indicated by common sense. With identities and antitheses the events are two in number, the identity or antithesis between them being the remote phase. With all of the more ordinary verbal quibbles (class I. of these jokes) of the least propriety of production, and with most jokes in any way appropriate on metaphors, what I call a "concomitant and incidental" event of the occasion is necessary, in addition to the permanent (or primary) event. Procedure not expressed in words may, provided it is fully definite, constitute an event of the occasion, but there are not many instances of this.

It is a condition of the propriety of production of the event or events of an occasion that it or they should have been produced in a natural manner; or, where there are two events, that they should have been brought into natural association with each other. At the same time * there would be no less wit—in the sense in which I use the word—shown by a person who discovered a phase of novelty when the event or events of the occasion happened to be before him without having been naturally produced or naturally brought into association.

The phases of novelty are removed from the ordinary mental range momentarily, or longer by reason severally of the following circumstances. As regards the phases of special connection, some are remote because it is not imperative on one to seek special relations between ideas (see identities

\* See, for instance, illustration No. 19, Chapter VI., Part I.

and antitheses); some because, while the phase of novelty is expressed, right reason (see puns), or convention (see metaphors and idioms treated from the risible point of view), presents another idea solely. The phases of novelty presented in verbal quibbles are remote because not in the direction indicated by common sense. Those contained in the events of the occasion not altogether but in one or more prominent features, are remote because ordinarily if the mind conceived any phase retaining the prominent features of the event of the occasion, such phase would be a fundamentally similar one, whereas the phase of novelty presents a fundamental difference. The phases having an invariable immediate class connection are remote because, while the phase is definitely presented by reason of the possession of that connection, it is either not the phase indicated by common sense, or not that indicated by the ordinary principles of human procedure. The phases of exceptional immediate connection, and not pertaining to external nature, are remote because right reason does not require us to look for the phase (the remoteness here being usually no more than momentary); and the phases of external nature, with exceptional immediate connection, because there is nothing to suggest a search for any remarkable phase in connection with the events of the ocasion. Obvious exaggerations are remote, because the mind ordinarily contemplates a phase in its true or approximately true aspect. The phases having general connections only, these constituting the rest of class I. and the whole of class II., are remote because in opposition to common sense.

And the necessary risible phase in one form or another, and in one person or another, caused by this remoteness (and specified at the beginning of Chapter VI.) gives, with further imperfection or not according to circumstances, a more or less risible aspect to every incident containing a phase of circumstantial novelty No. 2.

We see from the foregoing that the expression, remoteness from the ordinary mental range, implies a definite limitation * of the mind for the moment or longer to an idea or ideas other than the phase of circumstantial novelty No. 2. Supposing one on the presentation of the events of an occasion, to set aside such one or more of the above limitations as he may choose, and engage in the search for a phase of circumstantial novelty, our attention becomes directed to another quality than the above generic charac-

* Where, as with the phases of exceptional immediate connection, there is no special reason to suppose there is any exceptional phase connected with the events of the occasion, this circumstance would limit the mind ordinarily to the contemplation of the event of the occasion simply.

## AND CIRCUMSTANTIAL NOVELTY. 47

teristic which the novel phase possesses as a factor of one of the incidents of a group, in its turn belonging to the category of incidents presenting phases of circumstantial novelty No. 2; viz., the individual characteristic of difficulty of discovery, much or little, upon which of course depends the whole substantial amount of the ingenuity of the third species. With the whole group of puns difficulty of discovery necessarily can only characterise the events of the occasion (provided then by ingenuity of the first species) while now and then chance, obviating ingenuity, will provide a pun, viz., when in the ordinary course of things one has occasion to express an idea, and the first form of words that presents itself constitutes a pun; which the speaker as a rule would note, but of which he might never be conscious unless it were pointed out to him. Nor with the first variety of group No. 6, or with group (strictly speaking, a special category) No. 8, is there ever any difficulty of discovery of the phase of novelty. In various other groups, varieties, or divisions, the phase of novelty in an incident will be marked by difficulty of discovery or not according to circumstances.

As regards the causes of difficulty of discovery, and consequent appreciable value attaching to some phases of novelty, a proportion of them receive a definite amount of appreciable value under general conditions, while all receive an indefinite degree of value according to the circumstances of the particular incident.

Having now explained, so far as can be done without specific illustration, the nature of circumstantial novelty No. 2, the witting discovery of which, we have seen, constitutes ingenuity of the third species, I arrive at the other two species of ingenuity. Species No. 2, being the witting invention of any of the risible phases illustrated in Chapters VIII., IX., and X., needs no reference here. The chief forms which ingenuity of the first species takes are;—mother wit, the solution, as we may define it, of the difficulties more especially connected with every-day life; ingenious expedients in general of a practical kind; falsehoods not presented in connection with the " events of an occasion "; the invention of similes within the limits of substantially rational comparison, some with a risible, others with a non-risible subject of comparison; the production of metaphors; and—this being the one form of this species of ingenuity which will call for special reference, though, as it is connected with circumstantial novelty No. 2, the scope of the references will be co-extensive with that subject—the provision at times (in the case of puns, almost invariably) of the events of the occasion in incidents presenting phases of circumstantial novelty No. 2.

And here I may state the grounds upon which I think the name of wit might in a scientific analysis be reserved, as I have said I reserve it, to designate the discovery of the phases of circumstantial novelty having a special connection with the events of the occasion. Taking, in the first place, the word wit to be a term especially indicative of an absolute superiority, the reason is this—that it is only by the discovery of these phases specially connected with the events of the occasion—phases definitely presented, and from the momentary limitation of the mind, for the moment at least unperceived—that an absolute superiority is shown; the superiority being in relation to oneself on first contemplating the events of the occasion, as also in relation to any other persons at the moment of their contemplation of such events. For it is these definitely presented phases only which give that uniformity of condition for all persons alike as regards opportunity for discovery, which alone admits of the exhibition of absolute superiority,—these phases only which give every one an equal chance of discovering them. This is of course only a question of nomenclature, and it is a matter of indifference whether I designate the perception of these phases by the term wit, or by the more general expression, ingenuity of the third species; but for the sake of brevity I will adopt the former term.

To resume. All search, even though unsuccessful, for events having a phase of circumstantial novelty of the second description connected with them would be exercise of ingenuity of the first species, provided, that is, that some reasonable idea is discovered. Thus (taking the would-be punster's mode of proceeding) a person who, with an idea before him, seeks, in addition to the form of words first occurring to him for the expression of such idea, any other form of expression, and finds it, exercises ingenuity of the first species. So, too, would a person seeking some general form of words with a view to extracting from them a particular interpretation more or less remote from the ordinary mental range (a person, that is, seeking material out of which a verbal quibble can be produced); even if he failed in finding a general utterance, and merely succeeded in finding a reasonable idea. This much, of course, everyone can do. Unless, however, the idea discovered by the would-be punster or quibbler has a phase of circumstantial novelty connected with it, it cannot be utilised; while moreover, if the phase of novelty is appreciably difficult of discovery with the events of the occasion before one, a proportionate degree of wit is of course required to discover it. With almost all—probably all—puns, one's object is practically achieved when the events of the occasion—the pun, regarded solely in its first signification—are provided; the phase of novelty—the second signification—requiring a wholly immaterial degree of wit for its discovery, a circumstance rendering it unnecessary for the punster, when he has given expression to his sentence, to indicate its second signification to others: (if there are any puns difficult of perception, the jesters must point them out, or resign themselves to their probably passing unnoted).

Risible phases invented by one person, but the unwitting or witting exhibition of which is ascribed by him to other individuals, existing or imaginary, are, as I have said elsewhere, due to conscious invention, not the present species of ingenuity; but to this species is due that large category of risible incidents in which the exhibition of imperfection by one person is effected by indirect means devised by another; such as practical jokes of most kinds, hoaxes, the devices and practical deceptions which enter largely into the material of comedies and farces, and are met with here and there in humorous literature; it being, of course, the imperfection itself which constitutes the risible element in the incident. To this species of ingenuity also belongs the invention of obviously incredible statements (absurdities) not presented in connection with the events of an occasion; and such inconceivable propositions as are simple, not complex, and therefore could not be made seriously.

The nature of the evidence of ingenuity, more especially of that of the third species, calls for some remark.

The evidence is of one or other of three descriptions, according to the phase presented. It may be variable and indefinite. Secondly, uniform or formal presumptive evidence, (this being confined to a proportion—the greater proportion—of incidents containing phases of circumstantial novelty No. 2, and existing in virtue of the intrinsic nature of the incident, not depending upon the character for ability of any particular person). Thirdly, positive evidence, this being furnished either (a) by a person's assurance that a phase of circumstantial novelty No. 2 presented by him was due to ingenuity *; (b) by reason of the phase not being reasonably possible of realization, or being an inconceivable proposition in the shape of simple nonsense; or (c) by reason of its being a phase of intrinsic excellence, as it seems to me are all the

* Thus superseding formal presumptive evidence where that would otherwise exist.

ideas due to ingenuity of the first species, except 'events of an occasion," and the phases just specified under the heading (*b*). The evidence of a falsehood being due to ingenuity would of course only arise when the falsity of the statement was known.

To state the evidence shown with the respective species: With ingenuity of the first species it is, as I have implied, positive evidence as regards all ideas not being events of an occasion. With respect to these latter, the evidence is variable and indefinite; though with one group—puns—as we have seen, we may be almost certain that the events in any given incident are due to ingenuity. With humour by surprise—a division of the phases of invariable immediate class connection —the events of the occasion are probably in the greater number of cases provided by ingenuity. So, too, are many of the twofold events containing identities or antitheses between them.

Of conscious invention (not being invention of the fixed and uniform mental inferiority which, as I have before observed, often accompanies the presentation of a phase of circumstantial novelty No. 2) nothing need be said but that the evidence of ingenuity is indefinite, and variable according to one's opinion of the ability of the originator or supposed originator of the imperfection, actual or represented.

As regards ingenuity of the third species, uniform or formal presumptive evidence exists, with three more or less comprehensive exceptions, to be stated forthwith, on behalf of any person presenting* the phase of novelty, provided the phase is not a mental imperfection in the presenter, this circumstance acting as a disqualification for the formal presumption of ingenuity, and admitting only of such indefinite evidence as there may or may not be, according to whether one thinks the presenter was joking or speaking seriously. This formal presumptive evidence attaches to the presentation of the phase simply because we are warranted in presuming, and we know that as a rule it is a fact, that a person who presents one of these phases has made exercise of ingenuity. The presumptive evidence might be fallacious, as where a person makes a pun without ever noting it, or where a particular interpretation of a general utterance, which interpretation would be remote to persons in general, and thus possess circumstantial novelty No. 2, was the only one which

* That is, the person ostensibly presenting it, who may be, for instance, a fictitious personage created by a novelist, who has not, however, expressly indicated him as being fictitious; or some existing personage to whom the incident is fictitiously ascribed, while really invented by the narrator.

occurred to a given individual; but the rule would obtain nevertheless.

The three conditions under which the presentation of a phase of circumstantial novelty No. 2 is not accompanied by formal presumptive evidence of ingenuity, are as follows.—(1) The formal presumption being superseded by the positive evidence of the presenter's assurance that the phase was due to ingenuity; (2) Its supersession by the positive evidence which arises when the phase is not reasonably possible of realization, and thus necessarily due to ingenuity; (3) The formal presumption—the phase here being a statement of the presenter's own motives for conduct, a statement professedly of simple truth, not of ingenious invention—being nuliified (see remarks on apparent falsehoods, group 7, division 1) in virtue of the presenter being the one person who knows the truth.

As I have mentioned (though without particularising) elsewhere, of the phases of novelty whose production is not in conformity with common sense, many which are not contained in the events of the occasion require, to give an excuse for their production, a profession of the presenter's belief in the full propriety of the production. This profession is sometimes made in so many words, as in illustration No. 6, Chapter

VI., Part II., and sometimes in a less explicit manner, though no less definitely, as in Nos. 7 and 8, Chapter VI., Part II., and elsewhere.

The profession (which is an exhibition of mental inferiority—defective common-sense—if the phase of novelty is reasonably possible of realization, and a nominal falsehood where the phase of novelty is not of that description) is, as we see, made in one and the same sentence which presents the phase of novelty, and it is, therefore, important to remember that the mental inferiority, or the nominal falsehood, is a phase distinct from the one of circumstantial novelty. As a desirable accompaniment, though not an indispensable condition, of the presentation of one of these phases of novelty, the mental inferiority, if the profession takes that form, in no wise acts as a disqualification for the formal presumptive evidence of ingenuity in the presentation of the phase of novelty it accompanies, but is attended by the like formal presumptive evidence of ingenuity of the second species as regards itself. And the two formal presumptions in these cases, we see, stand or fall together, for if there is no profession of belief in the full propriety of the presentation of the phase of novelty, and that phase is presented merely as having a more or less sensible

## AND CIRCUMSTANTIAL NOVELTY. 57

connection with the events of the occasion, the evidence of ingenuity of the third species is positive.

As regards those phases of novelty contained in the respective events of an occasion, which are easily discoverable by persons in general, with or without the imperative obligation to seek them which (see the second class of puns) sometimes exists, there is formal presumptive evidence of ingenuity—of wit—on behalf of all observers of the events of the occasion, as being presumably persons of ordinary intelligence. The evidence may be fallacious on occasion, but the rule obtains.

Where a personage in a novel presents a phase of circumstantial novelty No. 2, and the author has not expressly stated that such personage is fictitious, the latter, as I have mentioned, is the ostensible inventor of the phase, and, as such, the formal presumptive evidence of ingenuity attaches to him. But variable and indefinite evidence of the novelist being the real inventor would be presented according to circumstances. Likewise, on an occasion when a person is credited by word of mouth with the presentation of a phase of novelty, there might be variable and indefinite evidence of the professed narrator being himself the real inventor of the phase.

# TABLE OF CONTENTS OF CHAPTER VI.

## CLASS I. OF PHASES OF CIRCUMSTANTIAL NOVELTY No. 2. (PHASES HAVING LEGITIMACY OF PRESENTATION.)

Part I.—Phases definitely presented by the events of the occasion, and contained in them wholly or in part.

Part II.—Phases definitely presented by the events of the occasion, but not contained in them.

Also ... ... ...

*Groups.*

{ (1) Puns. (2) Verbal quibbles. (3) Metaphors and idioms from the risible point of view. (4) Identities and antitheses. (5) Phases partly contained in events of occasion. } Phases of special connection with events of occasion. Discovery of these (not in all cases followed by expression) may be called wit (sub-species of ingenuity of third species).

{ (6) Phases with exceptional immediate connection. (7) Ditto with invariable immediate class connection. (8) Special category (Inversions of certain ordinary processes of jocularity) provided from Groups 2 and 7; some phases contained, some not contained, in events of occasion. (9) Obvious exaggerations of certain phases. (10) Obviously exaggerated similes applied to imperfections. (11) Phases of invariable immediate unlimited class connection; legitimate of presentation through license. }

Part III.—Phases not presented by the events of the occasion.

## CLASS II. OF PHASES OF CIRCUMSTANTIAL NOVELTY No. 2 (PHASES WITHOUT LEGITIMACY OF PRESENTATION.)

*Group.*

{ (12) Phases with invariable immediate unlimited class connection. } Phases of general connection with events of occasion. Discovery of these (necessarily followed by expression) is ingenuity of the third species.

## CHAPTER VI.

### SPECIFIC ILLUSTRATION OF INCIDENTS CONTAINING PHASES OF CIRCUMSTANTIAL NOVELTY NO. 2.

### PART I.

THERE are, as we have seen, two classes of phases of circumstantial novelty No. 2; class I. (the phases in which are legitimate of presentation) comprising both phases having special connection with the events of the occasion (from being definitely presented by these, wholly or in part, in a more or less latent form), discovery of these phases constituting wit, and phases generally connected with the "events." The phases of class II. (these being without legitimacy of presentation, and having merely a sensible connection with the events of the occasion) have a general connection only with the occasion.

The incidents are all risible in one way or another, there being, independently of whether the phase of novelty itself is risible, at least one imperfection—generic, as we may call it—common to the several phases of, as the case may be, a division of a class (the first division, presenting special connections, though not the other division, of class I.), the first of two large categories shortly to be mentioned, a group, or a division of a group. These generic imperfections, being of a wholly mechanical description, are without interest, and have but very slight prominence; and it is, it may be observed, this slightness of the generic imperfections, more especially in the first division of class I.—the special connections—which enables many of these incidents (provided the phase of novelty itself is not risible) to show so close an affinity with the non-risible ingenuities—the similes and metaphors—of the orator and poet, while presenting the difference that the one description of incident is risible and the other not.

Specifying the first of these generic imperfections:—the incidents of special connection present a common, a generic, risible phase in the shape of a perceptible falsification (adventitious inferiority, of Sect. 1, Class II. of imperfections) of an instinctive judgment for the moment or longer by the observer of the incident (or in certain cases, only by a person or persons imagined by him*),

* Where the incident is such that with the actual observer the event of the occasion does not precede the phase of novelty, the falsification is ideal merely, being the suggested falsification of the judgment of some person (oneself or anyone) with the event of the occasion before him, but the phase of novelty not yet presented.

that the phase (the phases, as regards the two events presenting an identity or an antithesis between them) immediately perceived on the presentation of the event or events of the occasion, is the only phase (or, as regards identities or antitheses, are the only phases) presented to the observer, or the imaginary person, as the case may be.

The two large categories I have mentioned comprise the incidents presenting phases of novelty whose presentation, however valuable they may be from any rarity they may possess, is not fully appropriate—not fully in accordance with commonsense—such phases being the whole of those in class II., and most of those in class I. (identities and antitheses, and puns, being among the exceptions). In the first, the phase of novelty is accompanied by the profession, mentioned in the preceding chapter (see the heading, Evidence of Ingenuity) of the presenter's belief in the full propriety of the presentation of the phase; a profession made to gain an excuse for presenting the phase. The second category is composed of phases which do not need this profession for their convenient presentation, and those incidents—though no one ordinarily would think of taking such a course—where the presenter, at the cost of circumlocution, stated his knowledge that his idea— more or less valuable from its connection with the events of the occasion—was contrary to commonsense.

The generic risible phase of the first category is the ostensible mental inferiority (imperfection of Sect. 1, Class II. of risible phases) which the foregoing profession constitutes when the phase of novelty is reasonably possible of realization; and, where the phase is not of this description—the profession then being not an ostensible mental inferiority, but a nominal falsehood—useless expenditure of time in making an assertion which no one could credit (imperfection of Sect. 1, Class I.).

The generic risible phase of the second category is mental inferiority, of degree short of defective common-sense, in the shape of voluntary departure from the region of common-sense in search of phases, actual, reasonably possible of realization, or not thus possible, but all beyond the province of common-sense. This imperfection would also be shown in those incidents of the first category where the profession of belief is a nominal falsehood; but it is, I take it, an imperfection which would pass unnoted in the presence of the other imperfection common to those incidents, and on that account I have not mentioned it except in this place.

Such generic imperfections as pertain to groups or sections of these will be specified when the group or section is illustrated.

## NOVELTY No. 2 (PART I.)

Formal presumptive evidence of ingenuity of the third species, as explained in the preceding chapter, exists on behalf of every person giving expression to a phase of circumstantial novelty No. 2, provided such phase is not a mental imperfection in himself.

The like evidence of ingenuity of the third species is also (without the phase of novelty being expressed by them) formally presumable of persons in general to whom a latent but easily perceptible phase of novelty is presented, as where a pun is made and the second signification left —as it almost invariably is—to be discovered by a trivial exercise of wit on the part of the hearer; or where an easily discovered identity or antithesis is left unexpressed because thus easily perceptible. One may miss a pun, or an identity or antithesis easily perceptible to persons in general, and thus the formal presumptive evidence be fallacious on that occasion, but it exists nevertheless.

A laugh following a pun, or the presentation of two phases having an identity or antithesis between them, would without doubt, we may say, constitute positive evidence—superseding the formal presumptive evidence—of discovery of the phase of novelty; and perhaps we should regard the absence of this non-verbal sign of recognition as an indication that the phase of novelty had passed unnoted. In such case the formal presumptive evidence would be presented only to persons hearing of the incident, and who were absent, and could not therefore tell whether the non-verbal recognition of the phase of novelty by laughter had been given or not.

I now proceed to my illustrations, the order of which has been shown in the tabular statement at the beginning of the chapter.

(1.) PUNS. The events of the occasion—provided either by ingenuity of the first species, or by chance, obviating ingenuity—are the form of words bearing for the moment at least only a single signification (or rendering) and reference; the phase of novelty being the second signification which the sentence—or, if the pun is an imperfect one, a part only of it—possesses, either as written or pronounced. The discovery of the second signification and reference is an exercise of wit (sub-species of ingenuity of the third species), of course of a wholly inconsiderable degree. Puns belong to the category of incidents where the events of the occasion are not brought into view till the moment of the presentation of the phase of novelty, and to that division of the category in which the phase of novelty is not perceived, if at all, till a moment after the presentation of the events of the occasion.

The second signification in a pun may be described as differing from that in an utterance upon which a quibble is founded—in that while a quibble presents a remote and fully sensible particular interpretation of a general utterance showing no ambiguity in the words themselves, a pun presents an ambiguity in one or more words of a sentence, either as written or pronounced. Perfect puns are those in which the sentence is sensible throughout, in whichever signification the word or words of ambiguity is, or are, taken; while imperfect puns are those which make gibberish of the sentence in its entirety when the second signification of the ambiguous word or words is taken. The requisites for a pun—the conditions distinguishing a pun from a sentence containing a word or words of ambiguity merely —would seem to be as follows. Where only one word is punned upon, the second signification must have a reference—as being a repetition or approximate repetition of it—to some more or less prominent word in immediate proximity to the sentence; a reference to some entire sentence, such as the question in certain riddles, or the first part of the answer in some others; or a reference to some non-verbal event of the time; the sentence when the second signification of the word of ambiguity is taken being meaningless as a whole or sensible—the utterance an imperfect pun or a perfect one—according to circumstances. Where two words are punned upon, this connection of the second signification with some word or occasion of the moment is not necessary if the sentence when the second signification of the two ambiguous words is taken is sensible, but where the sentence is gibberish the connection is required.

A word, speech, or non-verbal phase of the description I have just mentioned—distinct itself from an event of an occasion, since there is no phase connected with it which is definitely removed from the ordinary mental range—is what may be called a " datum " or " material " for the event of the occasion, by reason of its having some natural association with this latter. It is, except where the pun is upon two words and is a sensible sentence, this datum which alone confers upon any second rendering of an utterance its claim to one's attention—this alone which gives it its right to notice. I call it, therefore, an " indispensable " datum for the event of the occasion, it differing in this respect from material for an event of an occasion which, it will be seen, sometimes accompanies the incidents of group No. 4. The data are commonly presented in the ordinary course of things, but they may be provided by ingenuity of the first species.

## NOVELTY No. 2 (PART I.).

Puns may be divided into two classes, those utterances of which it is not imperative, and those of which it is imperative, on us to seek the second signification and reference. With the first class a form of words is brought into a connection with the data for the pun, which connection is intelligible without our looking for a signification other than that which the form of words would first suggest; and thus, since a person ordinarily uses a separate form of words for each idea he wishes to convey, it is not obligatory upon us to inquire whether a second idea is conveyed in the single utterance. With the second class the form of words is connected with the data unintelligibly as regards the signification first suggested, whereby the hearer is obliged, if he is to find an intelligible Connection, to use the small amount of wit necessary to discover the second signification and reference.

Of instances of the first class we have one in a pun by Morgan O'Connell. He and a friend were walking by the river Wey, and O'Connell's friend took a plant from the river, remarking that it was a very rare specimen. "It is an out of the way" (Wey) "plant, at any rate," said O'Connell.[1] The spoken form of words, "It is an out of the way plant," is in its immediately obvious signification brought into intelligible connection with the first speaker's remark, and it is consequently not imperative on the hearer to look for the second signification and reference, "out of the Wey." The datum for the event of the occasion is the circumstance of the plant coming from the river Wey. On a sudden change of weather being characterized as extraordinary, a certain wit, Henry Compton, said: "Yes, we have jumped from winter to summer without a spring."[2] Here likewise there is no obligation upon one to look for the second signification of a physical jump without a physical spring. There being two words punned upon, and the sentence in its first signification being sensible, no "data" are required here.

Puns of the second class are almost all in the form of riddles. In one description of riddle the answer constitutes the event of the occasion, while the question is the datum for the pun. We have an illustration in the riddle (which has to be taken, as regards the answer, in its oral form): When is a door not a door? Answer: When it's ajar (a jar.)[3] The first signification of the answer has no intelligible connection with the circumstance with which the answer is associated, viz., the question, and it is thus imperative on one to look for a second meaning which is intelligibly connected.

A proportion of those riddles which take the

form of "What is the difference between" (*i.e.*, what is the likeness with a difference between) etc., etc. present puns in the second part of the answer. Such a riddle as the following gives an illustration: What is the difference between a certain sacred cantata of Mendelssohn's and the *encore* of a singer in that work? The one is the Hymn of Praise; and the *encore* of the singer, the praise of him.([4]) Here, as we think at first only of the pronoun "him," we do not see the likeness to the word "hymn;" but an instant later we recognize the identity which, when pronounced, him has with hymn.

The data for the event of the occasion are the words, The Hymn of Praise, together with the words of inquiry preceding them; these lastly-mentioned words being, while not absolutely necessary as a part of the data, yet desirable, in order to give a definite meaning to the words "praise of hymn" in their second signification—in order to show the particular person "him" refers to.

Passing from riddles;—in Berlioz's autobiography he mentions a joke of his when giving a criticism of *La Foie, l'Espérance, et la Charité*, a work in three pieces, by Rossini. "His Hope has deceived ours; his Faith would never remove mountains; and as for his Charity, it would never ruin him." The second and third sentences belong to group No. 7, and are there referred to; but the first,

"His Hope has deceived ours"(⁵), is a pun. The word hope has the conventional meaning of a musical work treating of the subject of hope, and the strictly literal meaning of the mental quality itself. The word "ours" means our (the critic's) musical piece called Hope, and since the critic has not produced any such work, it is imperative on one to seek a second signification for the event of the occasion—the words "has deceived ours" (*i.e.*, "our Hope"). If the sentence had run "His Hope has deceived our hope," or "Hope," the pun would have been one of the first class, for then the sentence would have meant, His musical piece Hope has deceived our anticipations; thus leaving no obligation on us to seek a second signification. The datum for the pun is the first two words of the sentence, viz., "His Hope," which we understand as meaning the musical piece because this is the especial circumstance under consideration at the time.

The remaining puns of which I am aware belonging to this second class and not in the shape of riddles, are brought into association with some non-verbal incident of the moment. As with the riddles I have mentioned, the first signification occurring to us having no intelligible connection with the incident with which the sentence is associated, it is imperative on us to look for a signification which has. To write on a chest of tea,

# NOVELTY No. 2 (PART I.). 71

"Thou teachest" ([6]), is one of these puns. The first signification of this is of course the giving of instruction; but as this has no intelligible connection with a chest of tea, we have to look for a second signification, which we very easily find in "Thou tea chest."

Since with these jokes, unlike the riddles I have quoted, there is no intimation in words that there is an intelligible connection with the incident forming the datum for the pun, there is a marked want of grace in the production of such a pun. But if we follow Charles Lamb's mode of proceeding with the above pun in contemplation, viz., substitute the Latin for Thou teachest, *Tu doces*, this defect is obviated, apparently because the comparative unfamiliarity of Latin makes the want of intelligible connection in the idea of teaching less prominent. It is to be noted that *Tu doces* in itself constitutes no pun, since it has only one signification, viz., that of teaching, giving instruction, information. It is only a particular English translation of the Latin, viz., Thou teachest, which gives the pun.

In my preliminary observations in this chapter, and in my remarks in Chapter V. on Evidence of ingenuity, I have explained what evidence there would be of wit in the recipients of a pun. It remains to be mentioned here that the evidence of wit in the producer of a pun of either of the two descriptions of class II. would be positive, from the circumstance that he could have no rational object in presenting a form of words with a signification unintelligibly connected with a given circumstance, unless it had also another signification intelligibly connected therewith.

In conclusion it is to be stated that there is, it appears to me, a risible phase common to this group of incidents, in the shape of a departure from right reason (imperfection of Sect. 1, Class II.) in using one utterance to convey two significations.

(2.) VERBAL quibbles. These form two classes, a joke of the first being effected by the presentation, with expression, of a particular interpretation of general language other than that which common-sense points to; the general utterance constituting the event of the occasion, and the remote particular interpretation the phase of novelty. A quibble of the second class is made by producing a general utterance to which the principles of common-sense, independently of special collateral circumstances, would assign, and permanently assign, one particular meaning (which accordingly is the one which at first occurs to the mind of the hearer or reader), but another particular meaning of which, evidently representing the real facts of the case, is, without its being expressed in words, quickly revealed by special collateral circumstances attending the event of the occasion—the general utterance. This second class might be called inverted quibbles, the unqualified term being reserved for the first and more ordinary class. Illustration of these inverted quibbles will be given in a special category at the end of Part II. of this chapter, together with one or two jokes of group No. 7, in which a like inversion of the usual process of joking is seen; and it will be enough here to mention that the inverted quibbles produce the usual falsification of a momentary—though with this class not more than momentary—instinctive judgment in the hearer or reader; and that their whole substantial value is necessarily due to ingenuity of the first species—due to the difficulty of discovery of the event of the occasion—, a wholly trivial exercise of wit being all that is needed for the discovery of the phase of novelty.

Reverting to the ordinary class of quibble,—the generic imperfections attending this class, all of which are mentioned at the beginning of this chapter, are, (1) the above-mentioned falsification of judgment—common to all incidents with phases of novelty of special connection with the events of the occasion—in the recipient of the quibble; (2) a mental inferiority, of degree short of defective common-sense, exhibited by the producer of the phase of novelty in respect of the departure from the region of common-sense involved in his discovery and presentation of the remote interpretation; while (3) in a few instances the jester might profess misapprehension of the particular interpretation intended by the general utterance—profess belief in the full propriety of the presentation of the remote phase, a profession which, as I have said, is an exhibition of defective common-sense. This profession, however, though necessary in order to give an excuse for the production of various phases of novelty not contained in the events of the occasion, is not thus necessary with quibbles of any value; nothing being needed as an excuse for these beyond one or other of the two conditions, shortly to be mentioned, which give the phase of novelty an appreciable value.

With most quibbles the event of the occasion—the general utterance—is provided in the ordinary course of things, thus leaving the wit, much or little, exercised in discovering the remote particular interpretation, the only item of ingenuity in the incident. A general utterance, however, as observed in Chapter V., may of course be provided by special search—ingenuity of the first species. To this ingenuity necessarily were due certain utterances of the old Grecian oracles, which were devised for the especial purpose of including particular interpretations indicating opposite contingencies.

## NOVELTY No. 2 (PART I.).

There are two conditions, one or other of which is necessary to give a quibble of this first and ordinary class a definite degree of appreciable value (a generic appreciable value we may call it) implying a definite degree of difficulty of discovery; thus distinguishing the joke from the mere indiscriminate production of any remote phase. The first is, the phase of novelty being either diametrically opposed to the common-sense particular interpretation, thus completely reversing the situation; or being a complete negation of the common-sense phase; with, at the same time, no departure from fact, or reasonably possible fact. The second condition is the phase being a fundamentally different one from the common-sense interpretation, and made a representation of fact in virtue of some occasional circumstance accompanying the general expression and in open evidence when that is produced; while not being a statement of fact if the general expression were produced under ordinary circumstances. This occasional circumstance I should call a "concomitant and incidental" event of the occasion.

Taking illustration, we have a reversal of the situation, by what is a reasonably probable statement of fact, in a rejoinder made to Louis the Fourteenth by one of his officers, who had been importuning him for promotion. The King, annoyed at his persistence, had said, "That is one of the most troublesome officers in my dominions." "That, sire," said the officer, overhearing him, "is precisely what your Majesty's enemies say of me." ([7]) The common-sense interpretation of the King's remark is that of trouble given to him—a discredit to the officer; while the latter presents the idea of trouble given to the enemy—a certain reversal of the imputation upon him.

Someone, *apropos* of the asserted dulness of some sea-side town, asks, "Can't you have any fun there?" and receives the answer, "Such fun as you may take with you." ([8]) The first speaker's words comprehend fun from whatever source it comes, and thus present two particular interpretations, one indicating fun for which a person is not wholly dependent on himself, and the other, fun for which he is thus dependent. The common-sense interpretation is of course the former. The phase of novelty is of course one of those effecting a negation of the situation presented by the common-sense interpretation.

If we transpose the joke by making the answer, "Oh yes; but you must take it with you," ([9]) we have a somewhat exceptional form of quibble, the assent given in the first part of the answer forming part of the general expression, and the words

## NOVELTY No. 2 (PART I.).

"but you must take it with you" constituting the phase of novelty. To explain the form of the joke in other terms, the question and the first part of the answer constitute an affirmation that fun is to be had in the town—a general expression—, and the rest of the answer a remote particular interpretation thereof.

If, again, we took as the answer, or rather counter-inquiry, "You mean, I suppose, such fun as you may take with you," ([10]) we should have an illustration of the phase of novelty being accompanied by a profession of belief in its full propriety of presentation (it being not fully appropriate of presentation because not the common-sense interpretation), although, as explained, the profession is not necessary in order to obtain an excuse for the joke.

In Mr. Louis Engel's book of reminiscences, *From Mozart to Mario*, there is a story of a lady who said to a guest for whom she had provided a very insufficient dinner, "I have been very happy to see you here, my dear sir; when will you do me the honour to dine with me again?" "Now, at once," he replied, to her amazement.([11]) Included though this very evening is in the lady's inquiry, the idea of taking it for another dinner is particularly difficult of discovery, the whole tenor of one's experience directing the mind to the thought of some other day. The "concomitant and incidental" event is, of course, the insufficient dinner.

There are two very prominent occasional imperfections exhibited in this incident; parsimony exposed in the lady—imperfection in the shape of loss of dignity, taking the particular form of meanness—and a still more noticeable imperfection in the guest—also in the shape of loss of dignity, in the particular form of discourtesy—in his alluding to the lady's defect.

There is a quibble in the remark made by a votary of Shelley on hearing Mr. Matthew Arnold's prediction that the greater part of Shelley's poetry would not stand the wear and tear of time. Applying, or rather improperly extending, this prediction to the Ode to a skylark, the believer in Shelley imagines the Ode thus worn down by time to, say, the seventeenth stanza, and represented by that stanza in the anthologies of the future; when in another sense than the poet's, we may "look before and after, and pine for what is not."[12] The event of the occasion is the lines just quoted, the "concomitant and incidental" event being Mr. Arnold's prophecy as regards Shelley's poetry in general. An exceptional feature in this joke, giving it some special value, is that there are two remote phases connected with two general expressions, both remote phases relating to the same process, viz.,

# NOVELTY No. 2 (PART I.). 79

the prospect retrospect and yearning in the material, not mental, sense.

This is one of those incidents, sometimes met with, where the event of the occasion, although in contemplation by the *joker* before he discovered the phase of novelty, is only placed before persons in general at the moment the phase of novelty is placed before them. This circumstance of course is merely due to literary requirements or considerations, and in no way concerns the value of the joke, as we see if we alter the form of the joke so as to produce the primary event, the general expression, in evidence before people previously to producing the phase of novelty. For instance, wording it thus:— Does Mr. Arnold tell us that the author of the "Prometheus," the "Adonais," the lines in the Skylark Ode, "We look before and after, and pine for what is not: Our sincerest laughter with some pain is fraught: Our sweetest songs are those that tell of saddest thought."—That the writer of these will have the greater part of his poetry worn down by time? Here persons in general have the primary event before them without the remote phase, just as the other had; and the same difficulty any amateur or professional joker would have with the general expression in contemplation, without the remote phase, he would have.

As to the mode in which the primary event of the occasion came before the joker, it will be observed that it was not presented, as with the previous illustrations, at first hand; he having at first before him only Mr. Arnold's prediction that Shelley's poetry in general would be worn down by time, whence his thoughts travelled to the lines in the Skylark, lines discovered by ingenuity of the first species (wholly inconsiderable), if he was looking for an opportunity for a joke; in the ordinary course of things, if he was not at that moment seeking one.

There is a very noticeable occasional imperfection here in the shape of an inferior (permanent) production by the compiler of the anthology (imperfection of Sect. I., Class II.) ; a single stanza in a short lyric being in an anthology a peculiarly unsatisfactory selection to make.

It remains to be mentioned (apart from the circumstance—already recognized, and which has nothing to do with our analysis of the joke—that Mr. Arnold doubtless intended this lyric as one of the exceptions to his condemnation) that it is only an interpretation of the letter of Mr. Arnold's prediction which presents a portion of a short lyric standing, while the rest has been worn away by time: the spirit of his words is of course the rejection of large masses of poetry *en bloc*, and the retention of just a few of such.

Where convention allows to a word or expression a precise meaning different to its literal one, while retaining the fundamental identity, the presentation of the literal meaning just after the word or expression has been employed under circumstances pointing to the conventional meaning, would form a quibble. Thus, to refer to the joke by Berlioz already quoted (see No. 5), a trio of quibbles would be made by anyone who, after a reference to Rossini's *Faith, Hope, and Charity*, had been made under circumstances pointing to the musical piece, had inquired if his mental and moral qualities were referred to. These, of course, would be quibbles without either of the conditions of appreciable value.

(3.) METAPHORS and idioms treated from the risible point of view. A metaphor—a substitution of one expression for another in virtue of some general and prominent point of similarity between the two—is, literally regarded, though convention ignores that aspect, either a nonsensical statement or a manifestly incredible one, according to whether the expression construed in its literal meaning is conceivable or not. To speak of a person being one's sun or guiding star is nonsense, while to talk of a *souvenir* speaking to one of an absent friend, or to refer to a person as flying along the ground, are, where the propositions are not made inconceivable by the evidence of the senses, manifestly incredible statements, while yet presenting conceivable propositions.

The similarity between the above metaphors and the persons or proceedings to which they are applied, may be described as lying in the common properties respectively of giving pleasure in some form, guidance in some form, reminiscence in some manner, and showing great rapidity of movement in some degree.

Idioms, of which slang terms constitute a variety, are, if literally considered, nonsense, nominal falsehoods, or, as with the expression "To have a mind to do something," merely lax phraseology. For a person to say he is "up a tree" —a conventional expression for being in money difficulties—when he is standing on the ground, is a nonsensical statement, being contradicted by ocular evidence; while to speak of having "taken his hook," or "struck his tent," both conventional terms for leaving a place, or to apply the phrase, "up a tree," to a past state of financial difficulty, are nominal falsehoods.

Before the application of my theory to the risible treatment of metaphors is stated, a few remarks might be made respecting the features in a metaphor which are not possessed or shown by the object or proceeding for which it is substituted; (its dissimilar and subordinate features),

## NOVELTY No. 2 (PART I.).

considered in reference to the legitimate, the conventionally intended mode of regarding these figurative expressions.

A metaphor is only employed for the purpose of noticing—only for the sake of—one, viz., the most prominent feature in the actual proceeding or object we wish to describe, which prominent feature is also the most prominent one in the metaphor. Hence it is necessary, in order for the metaphor to be of use, that the less prominent, the dissimilar features or phases of it should not be obtruded upon our notice through any cause. And in themselves they are not obtrusive, if the metaphor is used under ordinary circumstances, since, unless we made special search, we should think of them only in their average aspect, an aspect in no way remarkable. (This average aspect is thus the one the dissimilar feature presents of its own accord under ordinary circumstances of the use of the metaphor.) Whence these dissimilar features, under wholly normal conditions of the serious use and consideration of the metaphor—viz., the ordinary circumstances of use of the expression by the presenter, and the absence of special search for exceptional aspects of dissimilar features by the recipient—take a subordinate place; and one is naturally enabled to ignore them altogether, from the time when he first became accustomed to these figures of speech. Under extra-ordinary circumstances of the use of the metaphor a dissimilar feature either assumes in consequence an intrinsic exceptional aspect, or receives from such circumstances an extrinsic one, and then these are the aspects it presents of its own accord. These aspects due to extra-ordinary circumstances make a legitimate claim upon our notice (though we may often pass them unperceived) as being both remarkable, from their exceptionality, and presented by the dissimilar feature in the wholly natural course of things, thus giving more or less propriety to the joke which the bringing them forward constitutes, though this by no means implies that the joke is always good enough to be worth producing.

To illustrate these remarks I will take two instances; the first one being in illustration solely of an exceptional aspect due to the first of the two causes, viz., special search, (for I know of no extra-ordinary circumstances by which this metaphor might be accompanied, causing a dissimilar feature to assume an intrinsic exceptional aspect, or conferring upon it an extrinsic one). The second instance will give illustrations both of exceptional aspects provided by special search, there being no extra-ordinary circumstances causing the features to present such aspects of their own accord; and of those presented of their own accord by the dissimilar features, by reason of extra-ordinary circumstances, viz., intrinsic exceptional aspects which these features assume in consequence of the attendant circumstances, and extrinsic exceptional aspects which they receive from them.

(1.) We have the metaphorical expression, the handwriting of Nature, as when we say, Nature has written honest man, or villain, or death, upon a person's face; the first of which I take for illustration. The metaphorical expression is the indication of character by manual penmanship, while the actual process for which the figure of speech is substituted is the indication of character by facial expression; the prominent and common or identical feature being the manifestation of character, irrespective of particular means. The precise means which the metaphorical expression presents, viz., manual penmanship, a dissimilar feature, take (means being of less importance than ends in their natural proportions) a subordinate place, in the aspect they present of themselves. For, there being no extra-ordinary circumstances accompanying the metaphor, the dissimilar feature presents of its own accord merely its ordinary aspect, of average writing with an ordinary pen, a phase in no wise remarkable. But if, making special search, we think of the exceptional aspect of writing with a bad pen, we have the dissimilar feature of manual penmanship disputing prominence with the feature of identity, and thus destroying the use of the metaphor as a figure of speech.

And it need scarcely be said, the production of the exceptional aspect at this cost of losing the use of the metaphor as a figure of speech, is only justified, only possesses any propriety, when some substantial counter object is gained thereby.

(2.) A person, in view of a long absence from an intimate friend, might give him a ring, and say, "It will speak to you of me when we are absent from each other." The prominent and identical feature here is reminding in general, irrespective of particular means; the precise means of reminding presented in the metaphor being the dissimilar feature of vocal speech. And, means being of less importance than ends in their natural proportions, the dissimilar feature takes a subordinate place if wholly normal conditions obtain in connection with the metaphor, viz., the absence of extra-ordinary circumstances of use, and the recipient's making no special search for exceptional aspects. The ordinary circumstances of use of the expression are the presumption that the ring will be worn on the finger, while the aspect the feature of vocal speech presents of its own accord is speech in an ordinary manner in every respect.

## NOVELTY No. 2 (PART I.).

As I have said, the two causes of prominence of a dissimilar feature can be illustrated with this metaphor. Taking the first, viz., the production of an exceptional aspect through special search, irrespective of the presence of any extra-ordinary circumstances, and consequently always an intrinsic aspect, we should have an instance in the production of the idea of the ring shouting, or another in that of its speaking in a whisper, another in hoarseness, etc., etc.; the idea thus, because a more or less remarkable dissimilar phase, destroying the use of the metaphor as a figure of speech, since it disputes prominence with the feature of similarity. The second cause of prominence, we have seen, is the presence of extra-ordinary circumstances of use of the expression, causing the dissimilar feature to assume an intrinsic aspect, or conferring upon it an extrinsic one, giving either aspect a more or less legitimate claim upon our notice, because both remarkable from its exceptionality, and presented in the wholly natural course of things. We should have an intrinsic aspect assumed, if, instead of the metaphorical expression being accompanied by the understanding on both sides that during the absence of the friends from each other the ring would be on the owner's finger, the expression was associated on the occasion with the extra-ordinary circumstance of evidence that it might reasonably be supposed to be at a distance from the owner, in consequence of which circumstance the vocal speech would assume the intrinsic exceptional aspect of a shout if it was to be an effectual reminder of the donor. This same extra-ordinary circumstance of use gives an illustration of an extrinsic exceptional aspect conferred; viz., the ring, while presenting its average aspect intrinsically, viz., speaking in an ordinary tone, yet giving an ineffectual reminder, on account of the distance. These likewise, as more or less remarkable aspects, destroy the serious use of the metaphor, through their prominence.

The foregoing remarks, then, will show us, by implication when not explicit statements, that there are two grades of jokes on metaphors—two grades of these productions of exceptional aspects of dissimilar features. Jokes of the first are the totally worthless and senseless production of the exceptional aspects which anyone can discover without the slightest difficulty on merely considering a metaphor literally, whensoever and wheresoever he meets it. Jokes of the second have, while not necessarily being worth producing, more or less propriety of production; these being of two descriptions. Firstly comes the production of the exceptional aspects (always intrinsic) which, while not being presented to our notice by the dissimilar feature

## NOVELTY No. 2 (PART I.). 89

of its own accord—there being no extra-ordinary circumstances accompanying the use of the metaphor—attain a substantial object for the producer; these, it would seem, always being jokes worth making. And secondly, the production of the exceptional aspects, intrinsic or extrinsic, which the dissimilar feature presents to our notice of its own accord, by reason of extra-ordinary circumstances of use of the metaphor—aspects which have more or less claim to attention because both remarkable and presented in the wholly natural course of things. While these latter are divided into jokes which are worth producing, and those which, though having more or less propriety of production, are yet not good enough to compensate for the loss of the serious use of the metaphor.

I can now pass to the discussion exclusively of the risible treatment of metaphors and idioms. I shall state in due course more categorically the conditions giving a joke of this group propriety of production, but I may at once mention that they are substantially the same as those giving a definite appreciable value to the quibbles I have illustrated. The like "concomitant and incidental events of the occasion" which sometimes accompany quibbles, accompany a large proportion of jokes on metaphors, (such events being here, the "extra-ordinary circumstances of use" of which I have just spoken); though it would seem there

# ILLUSTRATION OF CIRCUMSTANTIAL

are none such on the occasions of jokes on idioms.

As regards idioms from the conventional, the orthodox, point of view; since these present no subordinate dissimilar features, nothing need be said of them here, beyond mentioning that with idioms jokes which are difficult of discovery, *i.e.*, worth production, would seem to lie in one direction only, whereas with metaphors they lie in more than one.

A metaphorical or an idiomatic expression, possessing as it does the two interpretations of the conventional and the literal,* is a general expression, one particular interpretation of which, viz., the conventional, occurs to the mind ordinarily when the expression is used; and thus the notice of the expression in its literal sense may be considered a species of verbal quibble, the difficulty of discovery of the phase of novelty, however, being virtually *nil*, it being at hand for anyone who chose to bestow a moment's thought upon the matter.

Being though these notices are of the nature of verbal quibbles, I have nevertheless not described them as such in my classification, but for the sake of convenience have reserved the term verbal quibble for plays upon general utterances in the commoner sense of this latter expression.

* A literal interpretation of a metaphor would not, as a rule, express more than one of its dissimilar features, but it could of course be made to specify an indefinite number.

As with the verbal quibbles just illustrated, so in substantially the same way with metaphors treated risibly, for the joke to have such definite degree of appreciable value as to give it propriety of production (though this does not necessarily make it worth producing) one or other of two conditions must be fulfilled. (1.) The presentation of the remote phase—here always an intrinsic exceptional aspect of the dissimilar feature—must (as in No. 13) effect a negation—a destruction—of the situation ordinarily suggested by the metaphorical expression; or it would be more correct to say, must traverse the real statement implied by the expression. With these jokes, of which there must be a very small number, the propriety of production of the joke is not because of the dissimilar feature presenting the exceptional aspect of its own accord, in consequence of extra-ordinary circumstances accompanying the use of the metaphor, for there are no such circumstances: it is received because the production attains the substantial end of the above negation or contradiction. (2.) The metaphorical expression must be accompanied by, and reference must be made to (along with or before the production of the phase of novelty—the dissimilar feature in an exceptional aspect), those extra-ordinary circumstances which cause the phase to assume an intrinsic exceptional aspect or confer upon it an extrinsic one. The reason why fulfilment of this condition gives propriety to the production of the dissimilar feature is that an exceptional aspect which is due to the wholly natural course of things has obviously some claim to notice; though it depends on circumstances whether the claim is strong enough to be worth one's calling attention to the matter—strong enough to constitute the notice of the exceptionality of aspect a joke worth producing.

The extra-ordinary circumstances, as I have said, form a concomitant and incidental event of the occasion, the metaphorical expression becoming then describable as the permanent (or primary) event.

Proceeding to illustration;—Douglas Jerrold, on someone observing that Nature had written honest man upon a certain person's face, replied, "Then she must have had a very bad pen;" [13] thus, without leaving the other's metaphor, effecting a negation of the situation presented by the expression, a denial of the reality of the idea.

As I have said, in speaking of the feature of identity and the dissimilar features of this same metaphor in connection with the legitimate, the conventionally intended use of these expressions, the main circumstance of indication of character,

## NOVELTY No. 2 (PART I.).

irrespective of particular means, is the feature of identity, and ordinarily (*i.e.*, without special search being made for an exceptional aspect of a dissimilar feature), the one prominent feature, in the metaphor; the precise means of indication presented in the metaphor, (manual penmanship, a dissimilar feature) taking a subordinate place, in the aspect the feature presents of itself, viz.: of ordinary writing with an average pen. Here, however, through special search, an exceptional aspect, that of a bad pen, is produced, destroying the use of the metaphor, since we have a dissimilar feature disputing prominence, by reason of its exceptional aspect, with the feature of identity; this loss, however, being of course no serious consideration by the side of a joke like this.

I now take illustrations where the expressions are accompanied by extra-ordinary circumstances, forming concomitant and incidental events of the occasion; the metaphorical expression [then becoming describable as the permanent (or primary) event.

We may put in a more specific form a joke already given. At the parting of two friends, one gives the other a ring, which "should speak to him of the donor when they were absent from each other," and the receiver of the gift, or some third party, says, " Well, perhaps so; but it will have to speak up, considering the distance to the nearest pawnbroker's " (14).

The more general features of this joke we have already seen, and that an extrinsic exceptionality would be received by the dissimilar feature of vocal speech if we altered the version here given to the idea of the ring speaking in an ordinary tone, with the result of the reminder being necessarily ineffectual. I will now refer to such less general characteristics as the joke shows.

The concomitant and incidental event which the extra-ordinary circumstances constitute is, it will be noted, not expressed before, but at the same time as, the production of the phase of novelty (the literal interpretation with the dissimilar feature in an exceptional aspect). This does not affect the value of the joke, as I think will be evident if we suppose the concomitant event expressed before the production of the phase of novelty, as by some one saying, " You had better not give him the ring: he would only pawn it." There would be much the same difficulty in noting that there would be this exceptional aspect presented, as material for a joke.

The idea of a ring actually speaking presents imperfection of Sect. V., Class II. (ideal procedure unsuited to its nature by an inanimate object), but when the speech is a shout, an extra magni-

## NOVELTY No. 2 (PART I.).

tude is given to the imperfection, by reason of a loud tone for so small an object being especially unsuitable.

If a person were in very hot weather to employ the sun in metaphorical reference to another, it might with more or less propriety be remarked, "We don't want two suns in this weather." ([15])

The feature of similarity, and the only prominent one under ordinary circumstances of the use of the metaphor, may I suppose be described as the general pleasure emanating from a brilliant and luminous object, the physical warmth being a dissimilar and ordinarily subordinate phase. It is an extrinsic exceptionality which the dissimilar feature shows, as being unwelcome at the time, instead of welcome.

The concomitant event (the spell of hot weather) is not expressed in words until the time of the production of the phase of novelty (the literal interpretation of a second solar body, with a dissimilar feature in an exceptional aspect), but it was of course in evidence when the metaphor was used.

Jokes upon idioms of course present, like those on metaphors, two grades, viz., the mere worthless jocularities due to no more than the consideration of the expressions literally, independent of any question of special value from particular occasions, and those which have such value. There are only, I think, two descriptions of these latter; the first being those literal renderings which, when presented, effect a destruction of some presumably unwarranted position of superiority which a person has claimed for himself and expressed in idiomatic language; and the second description, the production of those literal interpretations which are in diametrical opposition to the actual facts of the case, and on that account are to a certain extent worth notice.

The first of these is illustrated in one of Lamb's jokes. Some one had asserted that he could have written like Shakespeare if he had had a mind to (conventionally, a disposition or inclination to); and Lamb observed on this, "So you see all that is wanting is the mind." ([15a])

Taking the other class,—a clerk in a public office in days when punctuality to the minute was considered something creditable, arrives duly to the minute and finds a fellow clerk of the same department as punctual as himself. "Our department's coming out grandly," says the first. "Coming in," says the other, in correction. ([15b])

(4) PHASES presenting an identity or antithesis between them. An identity or antithesis is of course an abstract phase, requiring two concrete phases—twofold events of the occasion—to fur-

nish it. While with identities there are all degrees of particularity, these differences are not found in antitheses, consisting as an antithesis does of the relations between positive and negative or approximately negative characteristics, or of a diametrical opposition between characteristics. There is, I take it, an exercise of wit in any apprehension of an identity or antithesis (whether the events of the occasion are expressed in such a manner as to apprise us that there is some identity or antithesis between them, to be sought for; or whether there is no such indication, and we are left to make the discovery unaided), by reason of our apprehending the two concrete phases in their individual characteristics only, for the moment; the wit being infinitesimal when the events of the occasion are so expressed as to indicate the presence of some identity or antithesis, and of varying degrees, from the wholly trivial upwards, where the indication is not made.

While, however, every perception of an identity or antithesis is an exercise of wit on this account, many of these phases of novelty would not be in the least worth attention. The condition which gives the phase of novelty that small degree of value necessary to repay attention (further, *i.e.*, appreciable value depending upon other circumstances) would seem to be the circumstance of both of the events of the occasion having an occasional or transitory character, in virtue of being actualities and in the temporal order of things. Thus if an employer were to say of his clerk, "His attendance at the office is as satisfactory to me as a heavy loss of money would be unsatisfactory," the permanency of character of the latter idea would preclude the antithesis from having enough value to repay attention. But if he were to substitute "his fellow clerk's attendance" as the contrasted phase, he would present an event of an occasional character, making the contrast worth notice. Again, if one said, So-and-so's hands are as white as jet is black, the notice of the antithesis would be worthless, because the second event, the blackness of jet, is in the permanent order of things. Whereas if he said, His hands are as white as his companion's are black, we have both events of the occasion of a transitory character.

An identity or antithesis, being a relation between two ideas, is not a phase which can exist apart from two ideas distinct from it, and therefore it cannot receive circumstantial novelty from these, implied as they are in its existence. It is, however, only abstract phases with which the idea of identity or antithesis is necessarily connected, and which cannot give it circumstantial novelty. When concrete phases present an identity or antithesis between them, the phase of relation receives circumstantial novelty alike with the remote phases in other groups.

The only generic risible phase on the apprehension of an identity or antithesis is the falsification of the instinctive judgment that the phases immediately perceptible on the presentation of the events of the occasion (viz., the two phases which these two events constitute) are the only phases presented. This judgment, however, is only an ideal one on those occasions—already mentioned—when the events of the occasion are expressed in such a manner as to indicate the presence of some identity or antithesis; such judgment being the conclusion—which I take it would necessarily be presented to us in idea—formed by some person or persons—oneself or others—on an imaginary occasion of their having the events presented to them, expressed, however, in some other manner than the particular modes which indicate the presence of an identity or antithesis. It would, too, it seems to me, be only on these imaginary occasions that the identity or antithesis between phases expressed on the actual occasion of their presentation in the manner I am speaking of, would be definitely removed from the ordinary mental range, and consequently only in virtue of these imaginary occasions that it constitutes a phase of circumstantial novelty No. 2. It is precisely because this mode of expressing the events of the occasion is only an incidental, not, as with similes, a necessary manner of presenting them, that we imagine to ourselves some one having them presented to him in some general manner not indicating the presence of the phase of novelty.

As to the modes of this indication,—it would be done in so many words when such phraseology was employed as "We may note an identity" or "an antithesis," as the case may be, "between," etc., etc. Such negative expressions as "without," "no," etc., are of course indications of antitheses. In such a case as a person's suggesting one circumstance in preference to another as a cause of some phenomenon—the phase of novelty here being of course an identity—there is something more than the indication of the presence of some identity: the particular identity itself is pointed out (see No. 16).

The occasions on which the presence of a phase of novelty is not indicated are, it would seem, those where literary considerations are adverse to the indication, and the phase is more or less easy of perception. And of such perception, as stated in Chapter V., there is formal presumptive evidence on behalf of the persons to whom they are presented.

There are two specialities, one or other of which attaches on occasion to one or both of the phases containing an identity * between them, and each of which, indicating as it does ingenuity of the first species, gives some appreciable value to the incident. The first of these specialities consists in one or each of the events of the occasion being a particular phase † of some more general phase which has been previously forthcoming. The other consists in one or each of the events of the occasion,—or it may be one of the more general phases just mentioned—being forthcoming, not from the general field of ideas (in the ordinary course of events, or by ingenuity of the first species), but through the medium of some phase which, while not in itself containing an identity with another, has some natural association with a phase which does, or, for the process is not always limited to a single transition, with a phase in its turn naturally associated with a third, which possesses the identity. These phases from which an event of the occasion is thus evolved (as I have mentioned, by ingenuity of the first species), I call, as

* The second of these specialities applies also to the category of antitheses, but I am not able to produce any instances of the first in that category.

† The discovery of the particular phase is ingenuity of the first species, not the third, because the particular phase is not definitely removed from the ordinary mental range. For, unlike quibbles and puns, there is here no one particular of a general sentence or word understood to the exclusion of the rest, but all alike are definitely presented in the presentation of the general phase.

## 102  *ILLUSTRATION OF CIRCUMSTANTIAL*

stated in treating of puns, " data " or " material " for events of the occasion ; in this group, however, not indispensable data, since, given a difference of circumstances, the event—or the two events—might be produced without the presence of the datum or data. The datum is provided, according to circumstances, in the ordinary course of things, or by ingenuity of the first species. In one instance (No. 16), it will be seen, a process of wit also takes place before the event of the occasion is forthcoming.

Proceeding to illustration, there is a story of two of the ancient sages engaging in a mental contemplation of the world, with the result that one was moved to tears by the phenomenon and the other to laughter. My illustration is provided by the first of these two events in conjunction with the remark, "The sage and the world!" (in quotation of the title by which the anecdote may be called). "Perhaps sage and onions was the real combination that caused the tears" ([16]). The two events of the occasion are the idea of a sage weeping at contemplation of the world, and the idea of that person in close association with onions, a combination which would also result in tears. The identity is, of course, the common power to cause tears in the philosopher which the contemplation of the world is asserted

## NOVELTY No. 2 (PART I.). 103

by the anecdote to have possessed, and which onions, we know, if placed near the eyes would possess.

The whole substantial value of this joke lies in the evolution, mainly by ingenuity of the first species, of the second event of the occasion, viz., sage (in the sense of philosopher) and onions, from data or material for such event furnished in the word sage, having as that word has a twofold signification. The first item of ingenuity (of the first species), viz., the notice of the second signification of the word sage, is of the slightest, if indeed the second signification is not suggested to the mind, thus obviating any exercise of ingenuity. A similarly trivial exercise of ingenuity (of the first species) would discover the idea of the frequent concomitant of the herb, though this idea, too, might not improbably be suggested, and ingenuity obviated. The third stage is reached by wit, for the expression, sage and onions, constitutes a pun, the second signification of which is philosopher and onions; and it is, I imagine, this step which would form the most difficult part of the evolution. Not being uttered aloud, but being merely a form of words passing across the mind, the words sage and onions would not make the special call for scrutiny which a pun actually expressed would make, and thus the second signification, philosopher and onions, might easily escape notice. When, however, the pun is noted the joker has arrived at the second event of the occasion. The greater proportion of the whole ingenuity required for the joke has now been exercised, but the same absence (for the inventor of the joke) of actual expression, which as we have seen would give difficulty to the notice of the pun in " sage and onions," would make it less easy to discover the identity between the events of the occasion than it would be after the special call for scrutiny which would be made where the second event was actually expressed.

It is, perhaps, scarcely necessary to point out that the word "sage," where we first meet it, viz., in the anecdote, unsupplemented by the remark necessary for the joke, does not make the passage a pun, because the story is not connected with any allusion to the herb sage; the word merely forms by itself an expression with a second rendering. When we meet the word a second time, viz., in the supplementary sentence, the words sage and onions form a pun, because the second signification of sage, viz., philosopher, is an idea shortly before presented to us.

We have both events evolved from data for them, in the latter part of the following extract containing a hit at the custom of furnishing houses in the Queen Anne style, and the practice of hanging plates on the walls; the data or material being (1) the idea of Queen Anne, and (2) a soup tureen on the wall, with two ladles above it. "But a closer inspection" (of one of these houses) "showed that we were by no means altogether on common ground with him" (the owner), "and that he had a life in the past which we could not share. The Chippendale chairs and the old blue china plainly showed the gulf between us; and in our first hasty glance at the soup tureen on the wall, with the two ladles above it, our confused imagination presented to us a death's head and cross-bones, as a sort of æsthetic crown and completion of the idea of mortality pervading the room, and associated with the memory of the late Queen Anne" ([17]).

From the idea of Queen Anne furniture (datum No. 1) there is a natural transition to the familiar saying, "Queen Anne's dead"—an idea of mortality—; while at a moderate distance a soup tureen against a wall, with two ladles above it, (datum No. 2), would have more or less resemblance to a death's head and cross-bones. There is thus furnished a more or less recondite correspondence between the Queen Anne furniture and the soup tureen and ladles, conveying, as each does, through a natural association or transition of ideas, an idea of mortality.

The soup tureen is of course an unreal exaggeration of the fashion of hanging plates on walls.

## 106   ILLUSTRATION OF CIRCUMSTANTIAL

In the next illustration the second event of the occasion is evolved from data, or material, for it; while the first is a particular phase of a more general phase previously presented. The passage is from *A Recoiling Vengeance*, by Mr. Frank Barrett. "Now the cocoanut was not a bad sort of fellow . . . Some people thought he was hard and dry all through, but they were mistaken, for there was some milk inside him, and it was the milk of human kindness" ([18]).

Speaking first of the evolutionary process by which we reach the second event of the occasion, we first have the asserted belief of certain persons that the cocoanut was hard and dry, taking that expression in the sense of moral hardness and dryness. A natural evolution from the expression of this belief is the presentation of the contrary idea, viz., that of the cocoanut being of a kind disposition. From this we are able to proceed to the metaphorical expression for kindness of disposition, viz., the milk of human kindness, giving us the second event of the occasion.

The other event of the occasion is the particular phase, the milk in a cocoanut, embraced in the more general phase, previously presented, of the cocoanut entire.

There is a decided license, which deducts from the value of the incident, and which we instinctively allow for in our estimate of its value, in

## NOVELTY No. 2 (PART I.).

asserting the cocoanut's possession of a "human" quality. And further, as the words run there is mention of but one kind of milk, viz., the metaphorical, so that it is only in effect—only by suggestion—that there are presented the two phases requisite for this group of incidents, viz. the material milk and the metaphorical, with a general identity between them.

There is an identity between a sluggard, with his slothful tendencies, and procedure which a person appointed arbiter of a dispute may take (the appointment being the "datum" for the second event), viz., the sluggard taking a special measure of sleep, and the arbiter doing the same thing ([19]); though their objects are different, the one taking the extra sleep in indulgence of his vice, and the other because sleeping upon a matter often secures better deliberation. The identity is formal only, not substantial, being in virtue of the process of deferring final consideration of a matter till after one's ordinary sleep being described in terms which bear the construction of taking sleep for better deliberation, independently of the regular and orthodox allowance. As observed at page 44, it is necessary in order that the notice of the phase of novelty should be made with propriety—should form a joke having propriety of production—that the two events of the occasion should be brought into natural association with each other, but of course a very little skill of adaptation (ingenuity of the first species) will effect this. We might suppose the sluggard himself to be appointed an arbiter of a dispute, when he could say, by way of a joke at his own expense, "This matter must be slept upon to insure better deliberation." Or we might suppose some one making the observation for him, in some such words as "You must sleep upon the matter to ensure the best judgment possible." Or, again, the sluggard and the referee might be different persons, but in each other's company on the occasion, when other versions of the joke might be produced, such as the referee inquiring if the sluggard does not envy him his appointment, in view of the excuse it gives for additional sleep.

In both this and the preceding versions of the joke there is the additional element of an unsuccessful attempt at deceit by the sluggard (imperfection of Sect. I., Class II.) in pretending to want extra sleep for the same object as arbitrators in general might claim it, viz., for deliberation on the matters before them, while he really wanted it as a vicious indulgence. In those versions of the joke in which the speech does not come from the sluggard himself, but is put into his mouth by another, there is, while not the reality of an attempt at deceit, yet the appearance of such attempt, upon the principle (see group 7, division I., first variety) of one moral inferiority (sloth) being a certain warrant for the presumption of another (the wish to deceive).

The next illustration is one showing neither of the specialities I have spoken of. In Charles Reade's *Double Marriage* is the passage, "Now this old gentleman" (a certain general officer) "prided himself on the neatness of his dispatches. A blot on the paper darkened his soul" ([20]). The events of the occasion are a blot on the paper, and the metaphorical expression, darkening of the soul; phases containing, not an actual identity, but a verbal one in virtue of the metaphorical description of distress of mind as darkness.

This is one of the occasions where, the phase of novelty being easily perceptible, literary considerations make it appropriate to leave the identity unindicated.

The undue importance given to the trivial accident of a blot constitutes imperfection of Sect. I., Class. II.

The remaining illustrations are of antitheses. Mr. James Payn, in *Holiday Tasks*, says, speaking of paterfamilias, alone in his house for a few days while the family are away, "The house, emptied of so much, is full of echoes, and its

## 110 ILLUSTRATION OF CIRCUMSTANTIAL

owner's voice returns to him without contradiction." ([21]) (that is to say, he receives, after an utterance, a return of his words instead of a contradiction.)

The events of the occasion are the sequence to paterfamilias' voice in the empty house, viz., the echo, which is a non-contradiction; and the idea (evolved from a "datum") of the sequences, in the shape of contradictions, commonly following his voice when the family are at home. This second event is not expressed in words, but is presented by inference, in the words "without contradiction." The datum for the second "event" is the circumstance of paterfamilias' speaking in his house on this particular occasion, from which circumstance it is a natural transition to his speech when the family are at home.

There is, we may say, even when one had arrived at the idea of paterfamilias' constant contradiction by his family, some appreciable ingenuity (wit) required to discover the antithesis between the two events of the occasion—the echo and the family contradictions—the difficulty of discovery being, it seems to me, because the fact of an echo being a phenomenon of external nature would tend to preclude one's looking for any connection between it and differences of opinion on the part of human beings. This connection it of course has in virtue of its being a reproduction of paterfamilias' spoken opinion.

The systematic contradiction which paterfamilias meets with from his family involves in him exhibition of imperfection of Sect. III., Class I.—experience of obstruction of legitimate progress.

In Talleyrand's remark that the English had a thousand religions and only one sauce ([22]), we have an antithesis with an approximately negative phase for one of the components of the contrast.

In the account of the "ransacking of a closefist," in *The Roots of the Mountains*, by Mr. William Morris, there is a twofold antithesis:— "They ransacked the house," says a carle, "and took away much gear; yet left some." "Thou liest," said Penny-thumb; "they took little and left none" ([23]).

The second event of the occasion—the statement of the truth of the matter—presents a risible phase in the exhibition of miserliness in Pennythumb (imperfection of Sect. VI., Class I.), made by this intimation of the scanty stock of goods provided in his house.

The following quotation from a burlesque article, *The Last of the Philistines*, gives a twofold antithesis:—"The fruits and flowers of æsthetic nature" (*i.e.*, external nature æstheticized) " were as mental diet, too much for them; as physical food, too little " ([24]). The words " too much " and " too little," it will be observed, give an antithesis in the shape of diametrical opposition.

(5.) PHASES of novelty contained in the events of the occasion, not wholly, but in some prominent feature or features. In this group the phase of novelty, while different in its entirety from the event of the occasion, is partly contained in it by reason of possessing one or more of the prominent features of the former phase. The remoteness—the circumstantial novelty—of the phase is due to a fundamental change effected in the situation (and to be duly explained); the mere presentation of a sentence retaining, while differing in other respects, one or more prominent features of a previous utterance, being, if it lacks a fundamental change, of course no exercise of wit; simply ingenuity of the first species, that is, if it is a sentence presented by way of jocularity, and not for the purposes of serious conversation.

The incidents form two varieties. In the first the fundamental change is effected by a single word or phrase which in the event of the occasion was used in one signification, being presented in the phase of novelty in another sense. In the second variety the change consists in some re-

## NOVELTY No. 2 (PART I.). 113

versal, real or ideal, of the relations between the parties concerned; such reversal being effected by the presentation of, it may be one, it may be more than one, of the prominent features of the event of the occasion (not used in any second signification) under radically different circumstances. The first variety may also present this radical change in the situation, and consequent reversal of relations; but although commonly required to give point to a witticism, it is not indispensable.

Where, as in No. 25, the second signification is not due to a difference of particulars under a general identity, but is owing to words of a wholly different meaning being spelt alike, the connection of the phase of novelty with the event of the occasion is formal only, not substantial.

Taking illustration of the first variety; in the opening lines of *Pearl and Emerald*, by Mr. R. E. Francillon, are the words, "Were I Rothchild himself, I would still say to all cavillers, 'There lies my glove!' And if they should reply that my glove is not the only thing about me that lies [25] —why, that is their affair, not mine." Here the word "lies" is used in different senses. The event of the occasion is, "There lies my glove;" while the phase of novelty is not the sentence following, but what that sentence infers, viz.,

"Your tongue also lies." A reversal of the relations between the parties is also effected by the joke, the air of boastfulness in the one speech being followed by the imputation of mendacity in the second. We should have the one change without the other—and, of course, a very pointless joke—if it had been said, "I am sure your glove is the only thing about you that lies."

A certain clergyman, speaking of some sermon by another which had been much praised, said, "I could have written one myself on the subject in an hour or so, and thought nothing of it." "And perhaps your congregation would have thought nothing of it, too," ([26]) said someone present. The phrase, "think nothing of it," has, from the word "it" being of a general character, the two significations of "think nothing (*i.e.*, little) of the trouble of writing the sermon," and "think nothing of the sermon itself." Here, too, we have a reversal of relations between the parties.

In the second variety, as before stated, the fundamental change in the situation is not given by means of a second signification in a word or phrase, but by the presentation of a feature or features of prominence under radically different circumstances. The condition of appreciable value in the joke is that the phase of novelty

## NOVELTY No. 2 (PART I.). 115

should be one that would be wholly natural of occurrence. Phases retaining a prominent feature or features of an utterance or of other procedure and fundamentally changing the situation are easy enough of invention if they are not such as are in the natural course of events; but the number of wholly natural ideas with the requisite connection with the event of the occasion is always small, the number being often no doubt limited to the one phase discovered by the joker. A further factor in the value of the joke is sometimes the extent to which the features presented in the first situation are retained in the second.

We will suppose a customer at a public-house where the scores are chalked up against the wall, viewing with some dissatisfaction his landlord's unfailing certainty in recording the debts of the former, and thinking, or saying, "Before long, I hope, there will be more chalk inside his fingers than outside,"([27]) alluding to the disease of chalk-stones. Or we might suppose him to say, "I wish the chalk was inside his fingers instead of outside" ([28]). The change in the situation, while its prominent features are retained, is that in the one case chalk appears as a writing implement, and the fingers are the motive power, while in the other chalk is seen as a disease, and the fingers as a subject of it. The joke is a very moderate one, but it fulfils the condition preserving it from worthlessness in that the novel phase is of a wholly natural description, and further, all the prominent features of the first situation are retained. If we take the remark, "I wish he had swallowed the chalk" ([29]), we should have only the one feature of the chalk reproduced, while the swallowing of a piece of chalk is not in the wholly natural course of events. And an idea still less natural would be presented if the chalk were too large to be swallowed, and the speech had been the expression of a wish that the chalk was inside the landlord ([30]).

The event of the occasion in these incidents, it will be noted, is a non-verbal one.

The foregoing jokes — convenient for the purpose of illustration — are a little wanting in the fullest propriety of production, in that there is no strictly legitimate ground, but merely some excuse, for invoking a disease upon a person for simply making a faithful record of debts. This defect would not be present in the case of a person discussing the nature and composition of chalk to a wearisome extent, and his hearer uttering, inwardly or openly, a wish that the chalk was inside him.

A person sitting down on a railway seat that creaked, observed, "Music without words;" whereon someone else, who doubted the music, while recognizing that a remark had been made, suggested, "Words without music" ([31]), thus exactly reversing the situation presented by the first speaker, while retaining the prominent features of his speech, which, with the creaking of the seat, forms the event of the occasion.

The phase of novelty here, it will be observed, is wholly contained in the event of the occasion, if we regard the words irrespective of the order in which they come; but since in the phase of novelty the words of the first speaker are transposed, the joke comes under the heading of retention of prominent features of the event of the occasion.

The fundamental change in a situation by the retention of a prominent feature in its general character, while not in its absolute integrity, is a witticism belonging to this group. An instance is given in Dr. Johnson's rejoinder on a lady's remarking that a piece of music which was being played before them was very difficult, intending, of course, the implication that it was interesting on that account. "Madam, I wish it had been impossible" ([32]). In the "impossible" we have retained a feature of the same general character as the "very difficult" of the first speech, the one being only a step further than the other. The change effected is of course that the one speaker refers to the performance as interesting, and the other as the reverse.

## PART II.

PHASES OF SPECIAL CONNECTION WITH—OF DEFINITE PRESENTATION BY—THE EVENTS OF THE OCCASION, BUT NOT CONTAINED THEREIN, WHOLLY OR IN PART. SPECIAL CATEGORY OF INCIDENTS.

(6) EXCEPTIONAL immediate connections. These phases, I have said, are of definite presentation on the presentation of the events of the occasion because they have, as being undesirable or else remarkable, an importance not attaching to phases so connected with most events of like description.

The phases of the first variety, viz., those relating to human procedure, as distinguished from those pertaining to external nature, consist of offensive inferences from speeches which do not in themselves convey any offence. The "things one would rather have left unsaid," which have appeared in *Punch* from time to time, supply two illustrations. A lady who has been absent from town for some time asks a gentleman what scandal there has been while she was away; and he replies, "Well, the fact is there has been no scandal" ([1]); a speech unobjectionable in itself, but bearing the inference that there was a probability or reasonable possibility that scandal depended on the lady's presence. Again, the host at a round table at which are seated as many

## NOVELTY No. 2 (PART II).

guests as it will hold, observes, "Mr. and Mrs. So-and-so were asked to come to us to-night, but could not" (²), whereupon each guest, noting the inference, thinks, "I wonder who of us would have been left out?"

These phases of novelty—these phases inferred from the actual words—are, as it seems to me, momentarily removed from the ordinary mental range because, right reason not requiring that one should satisfy himself before speaking that a sentence, innocuous in itself, has no offensive inference, the mind for the moment stops at the idea represented by the sentence itself. The inquiry before speaking which expediency, as distinguished from right reason, recommends, is a subsequent process.

The falsification of the instinctive judgment that the event of the occasion carries no inference of special importance is common to the speaker and his hearer or hearers. The speaker's additional error of judgment in committing himself to the speech is, of course, a more considerable imperfection.

There would be formal presumption that everyone, hearers and speaker alike, would discover the phase of novelty—the offensive inference—sooner or later, though here as elsewhere the evidence may be delusive as regards particular persons. (If the incidents were real, and personal assurances of their discovery of the offensive inferences had been given by any of the audience to any other person or persons, such latter would have positive evidence, superseding the formal presumptive evidence, of the discovery.)

The imperfections other than the above errors of judgment should be mentioned. In each case the speaker exhibits risible imperfection in the shape of discourtesy (imperfection of Sect. VI., Class I.) In the lady of the first anecdote moral inferiority is inferred in respect of her presumed love of scandal. And in some two of the guests at the dinner table, viz., whichever two would have been uninvited if the absent couple had been able to come, there is exhibited risible imperfection (of Sect. I., Class II.) in the shape of inferiority in one or more directions, mental, social, or both, to a generality of persons, viz., the generality of guests at the table.

The occasional phases relating to external nature which form the second variety of this group owe their special importance to their being in some degree remarkable. These phases are not, like those of the other variety, momentarily, but are permanently, removed from the ordinary mental range. When giraffes were first heard of, one of the comments on them was that they would be liable to seven feet or so of sore throat (³). Again, in, I think, Longfellow's *Hyperion*, there is mentioned a road which, if you followed it, was found to dwindle to a squirrel-track and run up a tree (⁴).

The event of the occasion in the first incident is the idea of the giraffe—of an animal with an extraordinarily long neck; and in the second, an unfinished road; the phases of novelty being the liability, or apparent liability, to sore throat on a most exceptionally extensive scale, and a vertical track as a natural termination to an unfinished road. And they are remote, as I mentioned in Chapter V., because there is nothing to suggest to the mind on contemplation of the respective events of the occasion that there are any remarkable phases connected with them.

The formal presumptive evidence of ingenuity would be present with this variety whenever the person verbally expressing the phase of novelty made no mention of his having met with it in the actual course of events of external nature.


(7) PHASES of invariable immediate class connection. There are two divisions of these incidents. In the first, the phase of novelty belongs to a class of ideas, any of which is reasonably possible of being, and one of which (presumably the one indicated by common sense) is, the real

immediate antecedent (in the shape of motive or cause), concomitant, or sequence, of or from the event of the occasion.

This division has two varieties, the first and most extensive of which is composed mainly of what we call improbable explanations. This designation would in strictness be applicable to the whole of the variety, but we commonly reserve the term, improbable explanation, for those incidents in which, from one reason or another, the probable motive or cause for the procedure comes into some prominence. This first variety I now proceed to discuss.

I take first those explanations which relate to another's, not one's own conduct. A substantial number of improbable explanations must be presented unwittingly by children, on whose behalf there is no formal presumptive evidence of ingenuity, these ideas when presented by children being of course not witticisms, but simply exhibitions of the mental inferiority, in particular matters, which is natural to childhood on occasion. Speaking with regard to adults,—as stated, or implied, at the beginning of this chapter (*vide* the enumeration of generic risible phases) where the presenter of the remote phase—it not being his own, but another's procedure which is under consideration—professes belief in its being the motive or cause actually associated with the procedure, he makes a fallacious exhibition of defective common sense. While if, though it would scarcely ever be done, he disavows such a belief, and presents the phase of novelty simply as having a sensible connection with the event of the occasion, he makes, by his entry into the region beyond the limits of common sense, a genuine exhibition of mental inferiority, of a degree short of defective common sense.

An illustration of these improbable explanations of another's conduct is seen in the suggestion, as a reason for a king's delay in making his appearance for his coronation, that the monarch had lost his crown ([5]). This explanation of the delay, which could be seriously given by a child, would be indifferent wit in an adult.

There is an anecdote of Henry Grattan that in a night walk in Windsor Forest he was apostrophising a gibbet, when he felt himself tapped on the shoulder, and on turning round, was accosted by the inquiry, " How the devil did you get down ? " " I presume, sir," said Grattan, " you have a personal interest in that question " ([6]). The motive for the inquiry which common sense indicates as obvious is the curiosity a person would ordinarily feel to know how a man supposed to have extricated himself from the gallows managed to effect that object.

Samuel Foote, the comedian, telling a story one

day at a dinner party, was interrupted by a guest (wishing to see if Foote could be taken unawares and put out) saying his handkerchief was hanging out of his pocket. "Thank you, sir," said Foote, replacing it; "you know the company better than I do" (7). The ordinary motive for such an interruption would be the wish to secure the handkerchief from loss, temporary or permanent, not the fear of its being stolen by one of the company.

The founder of Bentley's Miscellany at first thought of calling the magazine The Wits' Miscellany, a title to which the objection was made, by James Smith, that it promised too much. Shortly after, Mr. Bentley came to tell Smith that he had resolved to call the magazine Bentley's Miscellany. "Isn't that going a little too far the other way?" said Smith (8).

Here there are connected with the events of the occasion—(the decision to call the paper Bentley's Miscellany)—a class of inferences, viz., pretensions of the proposed magazine to the several degrees of merit and demerit which it is reasonably possible to associate with the founder of the paper, the degree indicated by common sense being of course that which attaches to a person of average intelligence.

As regards the substantial value which the joke possesses;—After a title of indisputable pretensions, like The Wits' Miscellany, a title bearing the name of an ordinary member of the public is necessarily brought into unfavourable comparison, and this gives an excuse for assigning to Mr. Bentley merits below the average, which excuse there would not have been under ordinary circumstances, the circumstances, namely, of the name of Bentley not being lowered comparatively by companionship with a title of indisputable pretensions.

Of course the ostensible beliefs in the full propriety— the full reasonableness — of improbable explanations, which are customary, are by the same formal presumptive evidence which makes them ostensible not real deficiencies of common sense, presumable, *i.e.*, suspected falsehoods of the nominal order. We do not, however, call them apparent attempts at deceit, from the several circumstances that the explanation is without the weight, much or little according to moral character, which attaches to the explanation of the person or persons who alone has or have positive knowledge of the true motive or cause; the circumstance that no material benefit would be gained by the presenter if his explanation were accepted on his authority; and the circumstance that common sense ordinarily protects the hearer from thus accepting it. In improbable explanations of one's own procedure—these constituting apparent attempts at deceit in the eyes of persons

## 126 *ILLUSTRATION OF CIRCUMSTANTIAL*

in general, though for any person having special knowledge warranting belief in the explanation (knowledge of exceptional moral integrity or other special circumstances) it would be taken out of that category—various special features are seen.

In the first place, no formal presumptive evidence of wit would attach to the presenter, by reason of the circumstance that positive evidence as to whether the idea is due to wit or is the simple truth, which supersedes formal presumptive evidence, can be given by the person whose procedure is under consideration, and is professed to be given by him. Evidence which we may accept in preference to his own account is, of course, special to the particular occasion.

Of course, knowledge that the explanation constituted a phase of circumstantial novelty to persons in general would be presumable of the presenter whether it was an ingenious idea in him or the simple truth.

In an unsuccessful attempt to deceive constituting a phase of circumstantial novelty there is an exhibition of the two risible imperfections involved in unsuccessful attempts in general at deceit, and referred to in Sect. I., Class II. of imperfections, viz., incidental inferiority in respect of an expectation, of substantial degree, real (to all appearance) or ostensible only, that the

## NOVELTY No. 1 (PART II.). 127

attempt would be successful, and adventitious inferiority in respect of a like and necessarily real expectation, of inconsiderable degree, consequent upon the fact that there must be some chance, even though infinitesimal, that the false explanation would be accepted. The number of serious attempts to deceive others with explanations opposed to the common sense of persons in general would, of course, be much smaller than that of those where the explanation was not thus opposed.

Regarding the incidents in their moral bearings, where an attempt at deceit is a dishonest one, and occurs in real life, any appreciable value which the idea may have for the intellectual sense can at most divide attention with the moral or material issues, so far as persons interested in these are concerned. While with jocular explanations the intellectual value of the idea is all that calls for consideration.

Where the attempt to deceive is dishonest the object of course is to present the most plausible idea, and it is not often that this has much value to the intellectual sense.

The events of the occasion are usually verbal, but where non-verbal procedure is fully definite it forms the event of an occasion equally whether expressed in words or not. A butler drinking his employer's wine, or a person taking out his watch and looking at it for a moment, are sufficiently definite actions to make it a matter of indifference whether the procedure is verbally expressed or not.

The former proceeding, expressed in words or not as occasion might determine, illustrates a serious attempt at deceit if we suppose the butler to offer the comparatively innocent, and improbable, explanation of the wine being drunk to test its quality, irrespective of gratification of the palate ([9]). The explanation would of course have to be one volunteered on detection if the procedure was not expressed in words.

The other proceeding—the glance at the watch—shows a jocular attempt at deceit if we suppose the owner to volunteer the improbable explanation of his motive being the calculation of its precise weight ([10]).

Where moral inferiority, or suspicious conduct, is observed, an improbable explanation of the procedure will have a certain appearance of coming from the person doing wrong or under suspicion, though it be put forward by the observer; as, for instance, where a person seen to take from a tree and eat an apple to which he had no right, was accosted with the words, " I suppose you think the fruit would grow better if the tree was thinned?" ([11]) or where it was remarked to a person carrying off something not

## NOVELTY No. 2 (PART II.).

belonging to him, that no doubt his reason for taking it away was that he thought it would be kept more safely for its owner if placed elsewhere ([12]).

This semblance of an improbable explanation proceeding from a person who has not actually made it, attaches because the presence or suspected presence of one moral inferiority is a fairly legitimate warrant for the assumption that another, in the shape of a desire to excuse the actual or conceal the suspected inferiority, exists; which assumption gives a natural appearance of the explanation coming, with the object of deceit, from the person to whose conduct it relates.

At the same time the wit in the discovery of the idea, as distinguished from the moral inferiority in the supposititious attempt at deceit, is credited to the actual speaker; formal presumptive evidence of wit in him attending the presentation of the idea, with the like evidence of conscious invention in respect of the profession of belief in the explanation.

Those taunts for obvious failures, which take the form of pretended approval of the procedure, are phases of this variety, the phase of novelty being, of course, a sequence to the event of the occasion, and the class of ideas to which it belongs that of opinions of the procedure.

A class of incidents, belonging to the variety,

in which a phase of novelty is—without being expressed—quickly revealed by special collateral circumstances as probably the phase of actual association with the event of the occasion—a class showing an inversion of the usual process of jocularity—will be dealt with in one category with what I have called inverted quibbles, at the end of this part of the chapter.

In the second variety of this division the phase of novelty is a sequence to the event of the occasion, in the shape of the expression of an emotion (or it may be, evidence of grounds for an emotion) in the person concerned, of an opposite description to that which according to ordinary principles would result from the "event."

In this variety the phase of novelty has a reasonable connection with the event of the occasion—is a reasonable, a legitimate sequence to the event—only in virtue of special circumstances, known (at the time the novel phase is produced) merely to the initiated, the reader being generally one of these. And to these, consequently, the sequence is not a phase of novelty (though it will be convenient here and there to call it one without stating that for these exceptional persons who are prepared for the character of the sequence the term is inapplicable), and no wit can be exercised by them in conceiving the

## NOVELTY No. 2 (PART II.). 131

sequence. As regards those not knowing, at the time of the production of the novel phase, of the special circumstances, for them to conceive an opposite emotion to the ordinary which yet forms a reasonable sequence, it is necessary that they should think of their own accord of some special circumstances which would make such an emotion natural. And since these circumstances necessarily would not ordinarily accompany an event promising a certain emotion, to produce, upon such an event occurring in real life, a joke upon it by means of referring to special circumstances which, in the generality of cases, would be found to be non-existent, would be too obvious an exhibition of the idea for the sole sake of the ingenuity to be appropriate. Thus, although whenever in real life there might possibly be these special circumstances accompanying an event, a phase of novelty in the shape of an opposite emotion to the ordinary is "definitely presented" to us, one can only appropriately produce the witticism by introducing it subsequently in some fictitious narrative form, with such alteration of accessories as would enable him in a natural manner to attribute to the special circumstances an actual existence.

As regards " evidence of ingenuity " in such a person ;—if on the production of the event of the occasion in real life he produced the idea of an opposite emotion to the ordinary, in the person concerned, mentioning the special circumstances which might possibly be existent, the evidence would be of the "positive," not "formal presumptive," description, since where there were no special circumstances already apparent, he must of necessity have imagined them, and the phase of novelty. If he introduced his idea in a professed narration of a real incident, there would be variable and indefinite evidence of the incident being an invention of his own.

As regards the person from whom the emotion would come; where, as is commonly the case, he is not himself the inventor of the special circumstances, while yet putting them in exhibition as real, as would be the case in No. 17 if a joke was meant, of course no ingenuity is shown by him. He would, of course, have knowledge of the novelty of the phase to those previously ignorant of the special circumstances; provided, that is, that he knew, as he commonly would, not excepting No. 17, if the speaker was joking, that the circumstances were special, and would consequently cause the emotion resulting from them to be opposite to what would ordinarily be looked for.

A remark is called for respecting the "generic imperfection" of falsification of instinctive judgment. Where the special circumstances become known to a person before the sequence is produced to him, thereby preparing him for the nature of the sequence, the falsification of judgment would not be exhibited by him, but by a person or persons imagined with the event of the occasion before him or them, without being cognisant of the special circumstances.

The incidents can now be illustrated. With the first, it may be mentioned, its representative form does not give the event of the occasion and the phase of novelty in the order in which the original occurrence would present them, the phase of novelty being given first and the event of the occasion after it; but one, of course, instinctively refers the two to their respective positions in the original order of occurrence.

A formal guarantee of an article is ordinarily evidence of its excellence, but under the special circumstances of its being furnished by a dishonest person it would indicate just the reverse. Being in itself only an evidence—I refer to the ordinary and reliable guarantee—of the value of an article, a guarantee is not a property capable of giving an appreciable emotion of pleasure so long as one is not in possession of the object to which it relates. But in the case of one's being already possessed of a thing irrespective of any warrant of its excellence, the subsequent production of such a warrant would ordinarily be a welcome circumstance. While on the other hand, the appearance of a guarantee known to be by an unscrupulous person would be the reverse. Here, then, we should have a phase of novelty to persons not knowing the special quarter from which the guarantee came. Such a phase would take its extreme and most striking form in the account of a person who had more than once, upon the faith of a written guarantee, given trial to articles from a particular quarter, which had turned out worthless, having an article offered him for purchase not as coming from any one place in particular, but standing apparently solely on its own merits. He examines it, buys it, and has, he thinks, every reason to be satisfied with his bargain; when suddenly he sees, what puts it beyond question that it must remain a dead loss on his hands, the written guarantee which he knows so well ([13]).

It is from what we may call literary considerations that in the narration the phase of novelty precedes the event of the occasion. We should have the actual order of occurrence if we read; Suddenly noting the guarantee, he knew that the article must remain a dead loss on his hands. The special circumstances, the previous knowledge of which makes the dissatisfaction a sequence only, not a phase of novelty, for the reader, are, of course, the exceptional experience of these particular guarantees being evidence against, instead of in favour of the goods.

We have a second instance if one said of some author that he habitually wandered so far from his subject that when his printers once put in a leaf from another work by mistake, it positively improved the book ([14]). The phase of novelty here is the resultant benefit from (through a certain license of supposition) what would ordinarily give the utmost dissatisfaction.

In this joke, although the special circumstances are stated in a general manner from the first, they are not completely indicated—we do not know the precise extent of the author's habitual departure from his subject—until the phase of novelty is produced.

Again, we may take the central idea in Mark Twain's account, in *The Innocents at Home*, of the visits, at some period of utter impecuniosity, made to him by a banker's agent, in the unavailing attempt to collect a debt. Calling regularly once a week, or oftener, he would plead long and earnestly for the money, or failing that, for something on account, the smallest instalment; and then, finding each time that it was just a case of empty pockets, he would remain, throw off the creditor, and settle down to a long luxurious conversation about everything and everybody. Under such circumstances as these the debtor came, and naturally so, to long for visits such as would be most unwelcome as a general rule ([15]).

A person says to a friend of his, an author of average ability, who has just published a book, "I never read any of your books I liked more." He then adds, "At the same time I am bound to say I never read a book by any other writer which I liked less" ([16]). This is one of the incidents I have mentioned where the phase of novelty is not an opposite emotion to the ordinary, but a circumstance (forming a virtual equivalent) constituting a ground for such emotion. It is the emotion a casual or cursory attention to the nature of the first sentence would produce, which here represents the "ordinary" one; the special circumstances being the knowledge which a closer consideration of the wording of the sentence would give, viz., that the preference of the book over all the author's other books is yet compatible with an exceedingly low opinion of its general value.

There is a story of a distinguished Impressionist being addressed by one of his pupils with the words, "They say there are but two names, yourself and Velasquez." "Why drag in Velasquez," said the other ([17]). To place on a separate supreme pedestal a painter not among those generally admitted as the greatest, and one other, would ordinarily be presumed to be certainly some gratification to the artist; but here we see the special circumstances of a most unduly high estimate, real or professed, of one's own performances.

To mention here a special point in connection with evidence of ingenuity; this is an instance, and the only one I know of, where the phase of novelty itself is (in virtue of the unwarranted conceit, real or professed) a mental imperfection in the presenter, and consequently would be precluded from carrying formal presumptive evidence of wit, however conclusive evidence of the variable and indefinite description there might be on the occasion.

The second division of this group is composed of what is commonly called humour by surprise; the phase of novelty here belonging to a class of ideas, any one of which is more or less natural or appropriate of actual association in the immediate future with the event of the occasion. This latter is, according to the description of the incident, an unfinished sentence, or a part of an obviously unfinished incident—for instance, a question without the answer. On the presentation of this portion of a sentence or unfinished incident, a definite expectation is necessarily formed, for the

## 138 *ILLUSTRATION OF CIRCUMSTANTIAL*

moment or longer, of a sequence to it of the description, general or particular, indicated either by common sense or one's knowledge of the principles of human procedure. The phase of novelty is a sequence of a different description to this, and the presentation of it therefore (or it might be, one's own speedy recollection that a joke may be forthcoming), effects the destruction of the expectation—a form of falsification of judgment. Hence the term, humour by surprise.

With one description of these incidents, the event of the occasion here being always, it would seem, an unfinished sentence, some word of general signification is used, first in one particular sense, and then again presented, to be employed, common sense suggests for a moment or longer, in the same particular sense, but, as we find actually happens, in another sense.

We have an instance in some lines on a bad fiddler:

> Old Orpheus played so well, he moved old Nick;
> While thou mov'st nothing but thy fiddlestick ([18]).

The events of the occasion—the passage up to and including the word "but"—point to the word "mov'st" being used in the sense of affecting the emotions, as on the first time of using the verb; instead of which it is used in the physical sense.

In the second and third sentences of the joke by Berlioz quoted in the first part of this chapter (see No. 5), "his Faith" is the event of the occasion in the second sentence ([19]), and "his Charity" that in the third ([20]). The phases of novelty have reference respectively to Rossini's Faith and Charity in the sense of mental and moral qualities, whereas the events of the occasion (though one may guess the description of the coming phases from previous indications) point to phases having reference to the musical pieces, since Rossini's "Faith" and "Charity" had previously been used exclusively in the sense of the musical works.

Taking instances of another description, two men were walking together, and one, pointing out to the other a person near them, said, "Do you see that man? Forty years ago he entered this town, purchased a basket, and set to work collecting rags. What do you think he is worth now?" "How much?" says the other. "Nothing," was the reply, "and he owes the money for the basket" ([21]).

In one of Mr. Burnand's jokes, the starter of a field of runners, after uttering the second signal "two," which is commonly followed by the final word "three," enters upon fractions—"two and a third; two and three-fifths" ([22]). The employment of more than one but a definite number of signals is a convenient process because by this means the utmost preparation for the several competitors starting at the same moment is ensured. That this object can only be attained by using a definite number of signals, common sense points out, and it would therefore be taken for granted that the final number "three" should be reached by the only process which constitutes a definite mode of progression, viz., integral numbers.

In thus delaying the race indefinitely, the starter causes in the competitors exhibition of imperfection of Sect. III., Class I.; experience of obstruction of legitimate progress.

Another illustration is the epitaph on a certain doctor, quoted in Schopenhauer's Theory of the Ludicrous, in *The World as Will and Idea*, "Here lies he like a hero, and those he has slain lie around him" ([23]). The event of the occasion is so much of the passage as precedes the intimation that the doctor has been an agent of death. The phase which would be presented to the mind ordinarily would be the general idea of some creditable performance, instead of which we find the reverse. The connection of the phase of

## NOVELTY No. 2 (PART II.). 141

novelty with the event of the occasion is formal merely, not substantial, the likeness to a hero being only in respect of the results of the work, not in respect of credit or fame attending it.

The illustration No. 23, Part I. of this chapter, gives, in the latter of the two events of the occasion—" they took little and left none "—an instance ([24]) of humour by surprise; for the ordinary supposition on hearing that little had been taken from the house would be that something would remain. There being no pause between the event of the occasion and the phase of novelty, one is scarcely enabled to form the usual judgment as to what will follow the event of the occasion ("they took little and left" . . .), scarcely enabled to apprehend the idea forming the event of the occasion, separately from that forming the phase of novelty. The place of the incident in this group is, however, obvious, and we have only to withhold for an instant the utterance of the word "none" for a definite judgment to be formed, momentarily or longer, that something would remain after the robbery.

The number is by no means inconsiderable of these incidents where, from the complete absence of any appreciable element of surprise, they have all the appearance of jokes which could not be classified with those where appreciable surprise is produced; but the community of the two descriptions is obvious when we note their composition.

In Schopenhauer's Theory of the Ludicrous, in *The World as Will and Idea*, there is quoted an anecdote of a Gascon who, when the king laughed on seeing him in light summer clothing in the depth of winter, said, "If your Majesty had put on what I have, you would find it very warm"([25]). Then, on being asked what he had put on, he replied, "My whole wardrobe." The event of the occasion is the Gascon's sentence up to "find it." The phase which would ordinarily occur to the mind at this stage would be the idea of a state of cold, making the phase presented by the Gascon—the idea of a state of warmth—one of circumstantial novelty. As with illustration No. 24, there being no pause after the presentation of the event of the occasion, one is scarcely enabled to form a definite judgment as to what will follow the "event," though of course a pause would produce the usual judgment in due form. And the incident presents a further speciality, in that when we have the phase of novelty before us we do not see how it has any sensible connection with the words preceding it. One would have therefore to make inquiry, as the king did. The answer, "I have put on my whole wardrobe," shows the connection (one perhaps only existing by a certain license, since the words "put on what I have" imply putting on a light summer suit. The expression "followed my example" would not be open to this objection).

(8) SPECIAL category: Inversions of ordinary processes of jocularity. I mentioned in the first part of this chapter a class of jokes which I called inverted quibbles; a joke of this kind consisting in the production of a general utterance to which common sense, independently of special collateral circumstances, would assign one particular meaning, but another interpretation of which (appropriate of notice because obviously representing the probable facts of the case) is, while never expressed, revealed to us by a moment's consideration of special collateral circumstances attending the occasion. I have also mentioned, in discussing the phases of invariable immediate class connection (division I., first variety), a class of jokes, belonging to that group and showing the like inversion of the common process. And these two classes from separate groups may conveniently be dealt with in one category. With the quibbles, it will be remembered, the phase of novelty is contained in the event of the occasion; while the phases of class connection are simply definitely presented by the events.

As with puns and various incidents in group No. 4, the event of the occasion is provided through the medium of data or material for it, the special collateral circumstances forming such material. And this "material," as well as the event of the occasion, is provided by ingenuity of the first species. The collateral circumstances are of a "special" character in virtue of their suggesting a phase other than that for the moment occurring to the mind; whereas the collateral circumstances ordinarily accompanying an utterance in the form of words the event of the occasion takes in these jokes, at no time point to any other phase than that which would be suggested from the first moment.

The data, it will be observed, are of the "indispensable" order so far as regards their being necessary to the possession of a place in this category by the form of words constituting the event of the occasion. Without the data, however, the form of words would still remain an "event of an occasion" with the same remote phase connected with it as here; in such case constituting merely an ordinary incident of group No. 2 or 7. Of course the context to the "event" would have to be totally altered, and the remote phase would be without the propriety of presentation which in this category it has from representing the probable facts of the case.

It might, perhaps, be thought that under my theory these collateral circumstances should be

## NOVELTY No. 2 (PART II.). 145

termed concomitant and incidental events of the occasion. The point is an immaterial one, but the following are the grounds for my not so regarding them. It is true that on the one hand they so far resemble the concomitant and incidental events accompanying the ordinary quibbles as to make the phase of novelty a statement of fact; and the circumstance that in this category the phase of novelty is the only fact connected with the event of the occasion, while with the ordinary quibble it is commonly only one of two facts, would not seem to be a reason for withholding the term of concomitant event from the collateral circumstances. The reason for withholding it lies in the fact that while both with the ordinary quibbles and with jokes in this category the accompanying circumstances are in evidence before persons in general, in the special category they are an almost certain guide to the remote phase—a practically open indication of it —and in the other cases give no assistance in the discovery.

Mark Twain's burlesque autobiography gives jokes from both group No. 2 and group No. 7. In this narrative—an almost uninterrupted chain of conceits, with here and there an unequivocal circumstance, in the shape of an obvious falsehood, completing the narrative—we have a relation, by inference, not expression, of continuous fraud and villainy on the part of the writer's several ancestors—with whom the story is exclusively concerned—in such a manner, however, that the several proceedings have a momentary appearance of being laudable, or else in no wise discreditable; it being by special collateral circumstances, not the respective narrations themselves of the several proceedings, that we recognize, a moment later, the true description of such proceedings. These special collateral circumstances are various common practices, customs, and ordinances in relation to crime; ordinances, etc., sometimes stated in words (as in No. 26), and which, where not thus indicated, a moment's consideration enables us (in virtue of a community of general characteristics between the phases of novelty and the ideas first presented to the mind) to connect with the several expressions.

An inverted quibble is seen in the reference to the ancestor who, having invented a patent gallows, went to see them perform upon the first white man hanged in America, "and while there received injuries which terminated in his death"[26]. This last sentence (forming the event of the occasion) would ordinarily receive, and thus we momentarily give it, the particular interpretation of some accident or wound in a brawl having been experienced; but the collateral circumstance

## NOVELTY No. 2 (PART II.). 147

of the gallows being on the spot when the writer's progenitor meets his death, immediately afterwards indicate, as the interpretation representing the actual circumstances of the case, the idea of these injuries having been caused by the gallows themselves.

In another passage,—"he was no sooner through with one contract under Government than they gave him another" ([27])—we have an unambiguous expression if we regard the word "contract" strictly, but with a slight license the sentence bears the two interpretations of a genuine contract, and a piece of any kind of business, before one.

I next take two illustrations of collateral circumstances revealing after a moment a phase of novelty of invariable immediate class connecnection—a phase reasonably possible of actual association (and here, because of the inverted character of the joke, the phase undoubtedly of actual association) with the event of the occasion. The first instance is a relation of procedure which, while really — as the collateral circumstances suggest—taken by the subject of the memoir in his own interest, has a plausible appearance of benefiting or being connected with the benefit of others; this supposed benefit being dwelt upon and no mention made of the self-interested motive. The passage is the reference to "the old Admiral," as he was called in the family, "though in history he had other titles." He "did great service in hurrying up merchantmen ([28]). Vessels which he followed and kept his eagle eye on always made good fair time across the ocean ([29]). But if a ship still loitered, in spite of all he could do,\* ([30]) his indignation would grow till he could contain himself no longer —and then he would take that ship home where he lived, and keep it there carefully, expecting the owners to come for it, but they never did."

Of course—speaking of the supposed benefit by the pursuit to such ships as were not captured—any extra speed in consequence of the chase would be more than balanced by disadvantages in other respects, but there is a superficial appearance of advantage accruing.

There are, strictly speaking, three events of the occasion in the above passage, and three phases of novelty, although they are respectively all of the same general character, viz., pursuit by a pirate on the one hand, and endeavour to escape capture on the other. The first two "events" are of precisely the same character, merely being expressed in different words, each event being a statement of benefit received by the owners of the

\* I have, it will be seen, continued the quotation beyond my actual illustration because of the fragmentary character this would otherwise have.

merchantmen from rapid sailing in consequence of the "old Admiral" following the ships. The third event — the words, "But if a ship still loitered in spite of all he could do"—is like the other two as regards the Admiral's following the ship, but speaks of a slower pace ; while the phase of novelty presents a like difference from the other two, being tardiness of flight instead of rapidity. It is only by a certain amount of license that unavoidable tardiness can be regarded as a form of loitering; but as the slowness of sailing is the essential feature, we are naturally able to allow this license. In the words, "his indignation would grow," etc., etc.—an obvious falsehood — we have one of the unambiguous statements which must necessarily be made here and there in a continuous narrative of this kind.

Another instance of collateral circumstances revealing a phase of novelty is seen where one of the ancestors is spoken of as having a "preference for striped clothes" ([31]), the prison dress. The class of ideas to which this phase belongs is that of immediate inferences from the event of the occasion — the having a preference for striped clothes. The inference for the moment drawn from this statement is that the striped clothes were worn in consequence of this asserted preference ; but a moment's thought shows us

150 *ILLUSTRATION OF CIRCUMSTANTIAL*

that they were worn in accordance with the will of the prison authorities.

This category presents the generic imperfection common to all incidents containing phases of special connection, viz., the falsification of an instinctive judgment — though not more than momentary in these incidents—by the recipient. The illustrations also present imperfection (of Sect. I., Class II.) in respect of an unsuccessful jocular attempt to deceive, not by a positively false statement, but by an expression whose particular interpretation, or whose phase of immediate class connection, suggested by the general principles of common sense, does not represent the probable facts, as revealed to us by the collateral circumstances.

## PART III.

### REMAINING PHASES OF CLASS I. (VIZ., THE PHASES OF GENERAL CONNECTION IN THAT CLASS) AND CLASS II.

(9) OBVIOUS exaggerations of phases of excellence or of imperfection, or obvious exaggeration or extension of conditions connected with the latter. For exaggerations of excellences, imperfections, or attendant conditions of imperfections, to possess circumstantial novelty No. 2, these three descriptions of phases must be such as the positive experience of persons in general, or, this being

wanting, such as common sense indicates are of appreciably less degree of excellence or imperfection, or are appreciably less exaggerated or extended attendant conditions of imperfections, than represented. It is the consideration of the phases in their true or approximately true character — their consideration in this lesser degree of excellence or imperfection, or this more limited aspect of attendant conditions — which forms the event of the occasion. While the phase of novelty is, as regards excellences, the exaggeration of the excellence; and as regards imperfections, in some incidents an exaggeration of the imperfection (with a second phase of novelty where the exaggeration has an accompanying feature—to be shortly more particularly referred to), and in the incidents where the imperfection itself is not exaggerated, the abovementioned obvious exaggeration or extension of attendant conditions. Both those phases of novelty which are, and those which are not, reasonably possible of realization are given legitimacy of presentation (the qualification, it will be remembered, for a place in class I.) by the laws of hyperbole, giving as these do a certain sanction to any increase of conditions already divergent from the mean.

Where the phase of novelty is not reasonably possible of representing a reality, as is almost always the case, there is of course positive evidence of ingenuity of the third species, while a nominal falsehood is uttered if the presenter professes a belief in its representing, or being reasonably possible of representing, a reality.

Mere increase of degree in the representation of an excellence or imperfection is a wholly mechanical process. Consequently, where the phase exaggerated is one of excellence, the incident, although presenting a phase of circumstantial novelty No. 2, is virtually without any risible aspect, the generic imperfection of defective common sense shown in presenting the exaggeration practically passing unnoticed. Where the exaggerated phase is an imperfection, there is, of course, risibility—in virtue of the imperfection alike in its real and in its exaggerated degree. But this risibility is of a wholly ordinary description, and is in no wise interesting. For interest to be given by an incident in this group dealing with imperfection, it must be either one in which, if the imperfection itself is exaggerated, some additional feature accompanies the exaggeration, or one in which, if the imperfection is not exaggerated, some attendant condition of the imperfection is exaggerated, or extended.

The incidents dealing with excellences seldom furnish interest, anything beyond simple and familiar exaggeration, such as calling a person

## NOVELTY No. 2 (PART III.). 153

"perfection," "the best," or "the wisest" of mankind, being seldom met with, since it would bring into prominence the generic imperfection of defective common sense in making the exaggeration, which the incident contains; and prominence of imperfection—jocularity—does not as a rule harmonize with qualities of excellence. Occasionally, however, something more than the familiar conventional phrases of exaggeration can be presented, and the notice of the excellence thus possess some interest for us.

Passing to illustration :—Exaggerations of degree, simply, need not I think be illustrated. Of incidents having more or less interest, I know, as regards excellences, of only one instance; the excellence being exaggerated, and the interest lying in a feature accompanying the exaggeration. Speaking of someone noted for his virtues, Robert Hall, the celebrated divine, said: "His moral excellence is such that if there were not otherwise room in Heaven, God would turn out an archangel for him" [1].

As regards imperfections, we have an imperfection exaggerated, and an accompanying feature presented, in a passage from Artemus Ward: "Shakespeare wrote good plase, but he wouldn't have succeeded as the Washington correspondent of a New York daily paper. He lacked the rekisit fancy and imaginashun. That's so." (²)

To speak first of the precise imperfection ridiculed, and accepting Mr. Ward's ridicule as warranted,—the fancy and imagination of these newspaper correspondents in its true degree—constituting the event of the occasion, and presented at the same time as the phase of novelty—is systematic misrepresentation of the description I have mentioned in Chapter IV. as being at once dishonest falsehood and thus an offence, and risible imperfection because easily detected, it being more especially in this latter aspect of risibility that it is regarded by Mr. Ward.

The exaggeration is made by representing Shakespeare's fancy and imagination, which no one would maintain, nor does Mr. Ward here, is below that of an average person, as less than that of the reporters.

The very considerable value of this joke lies in the humorist's representing a degree of fancy above Shakespeare's as in no wise remarkable—in his speaking of it in the ordinary terms appropriate to the normal possession of a whole class ; whence Shakespeare's measure of fancy, while in no wise diminished, appears in the light of a disqualification.

So far as words go, it is not said that Shakespeare's fancy is supereminent, and the reporters' still higher; the words would also admit of the interpretation that the reporter's fancy is not exceptional, and that Shakespeare's is below the average. But the reading naturally suggested—by reason, it seems to me, that there is a defect observed, natural to be noticed by exaggeration, and also because there would be no sense in under-estimating Shakespeare's fancy—is the former, that Shakespeare's fancy is supreme, and the reporters' yet higher.

The idea of the fancy of a whole class of reporters being above that of Shakespeare is a phase not reasonably possible of representing a reality. With regard, however, to the joker's profession of belief in its representing a reality, we cannot—the phase being not of the description which is contrary to the laws of nature—say with absolute certainty that particular individuals, even of education, might not really believe in the idea, and thus, although we have no reasonable doubt that Mr. Ward's profession of belief is false, such profession is not a nominal falsehood, but an exhibition of defective common sense, with formal presumptive evidence of ingenuity of the third species. We might, however, grant the contention that it must be absolutely certain that no educated person could really hold the belief, with the result merely that the joker's profession becomes a nominal falsehood, with positive evidence of the ingenuity.

Taking the second description of incident, viz., exaggeration or extension of some attendant condition of an imperfection, an instance of exaggeration is seen in Miss Braddon's *Sir Jasper's Tenant*. Mr. H. A. Dobbs, a confirmed joker, contemplating a friend with a very highly starched waistcoat, says: " A rise in the market price of starch may be safely predicted by all who behold Spinner's waistcoat " ([3]) The imperfection in Spinner would be, I should say, æsthetic inferiority (imperfection of Sect. I., Class II.), while the attendant condition exaggerated is the effect which the consumption of an extra ounce or so of starch would have upon the market price.

This exaggeration, like the previous one, is not a phase contrary to the laws of nature, and consequently the same remarks as were made in the former instance respecting the genuineness of the professed belief in the reality of the phase, would apply in this case.

An extension of an attendant condition is seen in Mr. P. W. Clayden's biographical work, *Rogers and his Contemporaries*. Quoting Mrs. Kemble, Mr. Clayden says, "Mr. Rogers stood before the offending edifice (a highly inartistic addition to Mrs. Grote's house at Burnham Beeches) surveying it with a sardonic sneer which I should think

## NOVELTY No. 2 (PART III.). 157

even brick and mortar must have found it hard to bear." (⁴) The imperfection noted would seem to be a certain want of dignity in showing contempt so largely by facial expression, while the phase of novelty, the item of interest, is the extension of the influence of the contempt from human beings, whom it might reach, to objects not accessible to contempt, viz., the bricks and mortar.

Irony forms a variety of this group, using the word irony in what it seems to me may be regarded its strict sense, viz., the indication to a person, by inference, not expression, of combined moral and risible inferiority in him, or, though this description of irony is found very rarely, of risible imperfection solely. It presents an exaggeration of the procedure noted to a degree making the exaggeration obvious to persons in general ; a degree sometimes reasonably possible of realization and sometimes not, but, in common with exaggerations in general, legitimate of presentation in the latter case equally with the former, by reason of the laws of hyperbole. Instances of this form of ridicule may be left for Chapter XI., where irony is discussed together with satire and sarcasm, by reason of a common element of moral inferiority being—with the small exception above mentioned in regard to irony—associated with these three processes.

(10) OBVIOUSLY exaggerated similes applied to imperfections—that is, similes applicable only to obviously exaggerated degrees of the respective imperfections, and thus beyond the limits of substantially rational comparison. These, it would seem, are phases of circumstantial novelty No. 2 in virtue of a remoteness from the ordinary range which the mind, if engaged in a search for a comparison, would take under natural conditions, viz., the range of substantially reasonable comparisons only, but which range convention probably more often than not prompts it to disregard when seeking a comparison. Almost all the amusing similes produced are of this description.

The generic imperfections are exhibition of defective common sense where, as is almost always the case, profession of belief is made in the full propriety of the simile, that is, belief in its being a true comparison; and, where this is not done, and the simile is confessedly presented as a defective comparison, mental inferiority, short of defective common sense, in respect of the voluntary departure from the regions of this lastly mentioned quality.

Except for the laws of hyperbole, these similes,

as it appears to me, would be without legitimacy of presentation, by reason of their not being substantially reasonable comparisons. Under these laws, however, they receive legitimacy of presentation; not, as it seems to me, in a direct manner, but indirectly in virtue of the object of comparison being legitimate of presentation in whatever degree of exaggeration.

(11) ILLUSTRATION No. 6, Chapter XI.,—given there because of the example of sarcasm which the incident affords—is the only incident ([5]) I know of exemplifying the group, in this class, of phases of invariable immediate unlimited * class connection; phases not reasonably possible of representing a reality and thus not definitely presented by the events of the occasion, but having legitimacy of presentation by reason of the extravagance of imagination permitted by the laws of ridicule.

## CLASS II.

(12) IN the incidents composing class II., the phase of novelty has a more or less sensible connection with the event of the occasion, but is without legitimacy of presentation from its being either (1) beyond the limits of reasonable possibility of realization and not receiving legitimacy of presentation from being sanctioned by the

* For the precise sense in which this word is used, see class II.

general laws of ridicule, or from being an exaggeration by way of irony or otherwise (when the laws of hyperbole give it legitimacy of presentation, whether it be reasonably possible of realization or not), or (2) a phase which is a reality but is altogether inappropriate of presentation.

This class, it would seem, contains only one group of incidents, viz., those in which the phase of novelty has an invariable immediate unlimited class connection with the event of the occasion, this term being used to embrace all those phases of invariable immediate class connection which have some sensible connection with the events of the occasion, while not being reasonably possible of realization, or while being realities, in any way appropriate of presentation. Such of these phases, however—as already implied—as have legitimacy of presentation under the laws of ridicule or of hyperbole, take place in class I.

The phases form, like the group in class I., two divisions, improbable explanations constituting the first, and what we may call worthless surprises, the second. Illustrations of the first division are seen in a passage from a work by Claude Tillier, a French humorist and satiric writer. A certain bishop, on a visitation, arrives at the house of one of his clergy an hour too soon; and as explanation of the cause of this cir-

# NOVELTY No. 2 (PART III.). 161

cumstance we have offered the ideas of the Devil having put forward the bishop's watch, ([6]) or the horses making unaccustomed speed from knowing the importance of the person behind them ([7]).

In illustration of the second division we may alter one or two of the incidents of humour by surprise in class I. We can suppose the starter of a field of runners—illustration No. 22, Part II.—to say, after "one, two," not two-and-a-half, but some number above three ([8]). Such a phase is not legitimate, in virtue of being wholly inappropriate, of presentation, since by no possible principles can an excuse be found for preceding the number three by a higher one. Again, if the inquiry—No. 21, Part II.—" What do you think that man is worth?" had been followed by the mention of some impossibly large amount ([9]), we should have a phase without legitimacy of presentation, because it is not possible of representing a reality.

# CHAPTER VII.

### ILLUSTRATION OF CIRCUMSTANTIAL NOVELTY NO. 1.

CIRCUMSTANTIAL novelty No. 1, it will be remembered, is a novelty attaching on occasion to certain mental inferiorities by reason of the existence of an excuse for the imperfection. The phases possessing this novelty may be divided into two classes. The particular description of the first class, which is much the larger of the two, is the accompaniment of the mental inferiority, which is usually of considerable magnitude, by some excuse for the error, or by some circumstance of the nature of an excuse, the former of which makes the error in reality, and the latter gives it some appearance of being, wholly natural of production, that is to say, wholly natural of serious exhibition by a person either in full possession of all his faculties at the time, or in possession of them to such extent as precludes total absence of mind.

The excuse, or circumstance of the nature of one, in this first class, is of two descriptions, the first consisting in some principle applicable in general features to the imperfection, and to that extent correctly apprehended by the exhibitor of the imperfection, but not applicable to it in its particular features; or in some occasional circumstance, involving no imperfection in the exhibitor of the risible phase produced, and corresponding with it in general but not in particular features. An excuse of this description may be called a circumstance of general affinity with the imperfection. The second description of excuse consists in the imperfection being the result of procedure which under ordinary circumstances would involve no imperfection, or but an inconsiderable degree of it. Of course for the observer to apprehend the circumstantial novelty of the imperfection, it is necessary that he should perceive the excuse, or—though the one word excuse may be used for both—the circumstance allied to it. It is, however, usually quite obvious, and indeed is sometimes presented by the situation itself.

As regards the degrees of value of the incidents of this class, these it would seem are determined, sometimes by the degree of the imperfection, and sometimes by the strength of the excuse.

Taking in illustration imperfections with excuses of the first description, and being in reality wholly natural of serious production, we have an instance, though the excuse is of the weakest, in Sir John Falstaff's answer to the Chief Justice when accused of living in great infamy : " He that buckles him in my belt cannot live in less." ([1]) The imperfection is the defective common-sense (Sect. 1, Class II. of imperfection) shown in the supposition professed that a stout person is justified in living infamously; while the circumstance of general affinity with the imperfection is the fact that stout persons are not to be judged in all respects like those of average girth. The principle, however, does not give the particular exemption Sir John claims, viz., exemption from censure for living in infamy.

A gentleman whose watch had stopped, made the remark that he must have it cleaned. " Oh, no, papa," said one of the children, " I'm sure it can't want cleaning, for I cleaned it myself this morning with soap and water." ([2]) Here the mistake is in cleaning a watch as one would the hands or face (of the individual, not of the watch itself). Minute particles of soap, which would not enter into the calculations of the youthful amateur, would derange the machinery, and it is a reasonable presumption that a very definite proportion of the towel was left to play a part in the watch's interior. The excuse for the error is in the fact that soap and water are commonly used for cleaning purposes, whence a child's mind might suppose they were efficacious for cleaning anything.

A person of precise and formal tendencies desiring a child when speaking of a dickybird to use the word "Richardbird," ([3]) commits error in supposing that the prefix "dicky" is used for the sake of its signification, viz., a particular proper name, whereas it is really used only on account of the euphony and familiarity of expression; whereby to give the signification by the use of the orthographically correct word Richard, by which the euphony and familiarity of aspect in the word dicky are lost, serves no purpose whatever. The excuse for the error is the circumstance, of general affinity with the imperfection, that if this familiar abbreviation were not used in this exceptional connection, but under ordinary circumstances, it would be reasonable to prefer the correct word to the abbreviation.

In *A Family Affair*, by the late Hugh Conway, Frank Carruthers, for some purpose of illustration, ascribes to certain pieces of bread the personalities of James the First and his descendants through the female side; a proceeding which, although it is strictly a nonsensical statement, is conventionally regarded as non-risible from its serving a rational object, that of facilitating explanation. Subsequently, however, we read that presently the butler came in " and swept away James the First and his descendants through the female side." (⁴) This latter statement is a risible item of nonsense, the fictitious personalities being retained when the occasion giving the employment of the nonsense its conventional rationality has passed away, the occasion on which the bread is secondly spoken of being one calling for mention of the pieces in no other than their actual character. The imperfection constituting the phase of circumstantial novelty No. 1 is the novelist's ostensible impression that a reference to the pieces of bread as James the First and his descendants is here also sanctioned by convention—is here also a non-risible (instead of a risible) item of nonsense; the excuse being the circumstance, having a general affinity with the imperfection, that at a previous time the pieces of bread were appropriately called James the First and his descendants.

We have two phases of this class in a reflection, or rather professed reflection, with which I was once favoured, and which I give here, concerning the attitude in which a joke on a metaphor—destroying as it would the value of the expression as a figure of speech—might be received by the abstraction Convention, as the ordainer or approver of metaphors as figurative expressions. "Extorting possibly," I quote from my friend's remarks, omitting context, "a reluctant admiration even from Convention herself. 'It is not a remark,' we can imagine Convention saying, 'of which I altogether approve, for you know I am concerned in the expressions such as you have jested upon being useful as figures of speech, but I will not deny that the idea shows ingenuity.'" [5]

This passage will serve at the same time as an instance of one of the many varieties of dry humour; though it takes but a very moderate position in the matter of value.

The first of the two phases of novelty consists in the speaker's supposing that the abstraction Convention—whom he assumes has the capacity of recognizing the merit of a joke on a metaphor —has, by reason of her being the authorised ordainer or approver of metaphors, an individual bias in favour of, a personal interest in, the retention of the orthodox use of the figure of speech, and consequent exclusion of a joke upon it; instead of impartially weighing the value of the joke against the value of the serious use of the metaphor. It is needless to say that if we do not regard Convention as an entity having no other existence but that of a president over the orthodox use of metaphors, in which case she would disapprove of a joke *in toto*,—and the exhibitor of this imperfection does not thus regard her, since he supposes her as taking some pleasure in the joke,—Convention has no such bias. For under these circumstances Convention is simply an expression representing the interests in one direction (that of metaphors) of persons—Society in general—who have also, as in the appreciation of jokes, interests in others; interests which, whatever the direction may be, are impartial—are in proportion to the intrinsic value of the production. To state the excuse for the imperfection;—The exhibitor of course recognizes that Convention, the president over metaphors in their serious use, represents a single interest only of a Society which has various interests. And he recognizes that the interest of individual members of Society—himself or another person—in the serious use of metaphors, is quite unbiassed. But the designation of this interest of Society by the term Convention—a special title, and with, if we like, a capital C—while no evidence of its being in reality a more important interest than that which Society has in jokes, gives a certain appearance of its being, although only one of various interests, yet more important than those not thus honoured; is a circumstance of general affinity with a real importance.

To speak now of the second phase of novelty,—the passage is worded, it will be observed, as if the joke spoken of was the first confliction with the ordinance of metaphor which Convention had ever met with. It is this erroneous supposition that forms the phase of novelty.

## CIRCUMSTANTIAL NOVELTY No. 1.

The fact of there being on the occasion calling forth this reflection, no positive mention of any joke but the one in question having been placed before Convention, forms a phase of general similarity to—and thus excusing—the assumption that Convention has had no such experience (an assumption which could not be naturally made of any human being, but which can be so made when we take humanity's collective interest in one direction and call it Convention, notwithstanding we credit her with humanity's general powers of perception,—ascribing to her, as we do, power to recognize ingenuity in a joke).

The phraseology by which this second item of circumstantial novelty is exhibited, is, like most intentional humour whose value does not consist in brilliance or richness, more or less insidiously worded, is the very opposite of a clear indication of where the imperfection lies. The imperfection is found in the words "altogether" and "I will not deny." The word "altogether," while by no means a clear indication that Convention is in doubt what precise degree of approval to give an idea conflicting with her ordinance but at the same time showing ingenuity, yet implies that she had this doubt; a state of mind of course incompatible with any general experience of jocular ingenuity conflicting with a serious ordinance. And "I will not deny" (that the idea shows ingenuity), while being in no way a clear indication that she thinks she might more or less properly refuse to consider any degree of ingenuity a justification for a remark conflicting with an established ordinance like metaphor, yet implies this—is equivalent to "I might refuse" (she knowing, our humorist supposes, nothing of joking being an established practice) "even to look at your idea from the point of view of what ingenuity it may have."

There is an anecdote of Charles Lamb being stopped one morning on his way to the city by Coleridge, who proceeded to commit what we may call a metaphysical assault upon him. Lamb, whose interests for more than one reason lay in the direction of escape, ingeniously cut off the button wherewith Coleridge had apparently secured him for a permanency, and, unnoted by the other, went his way. Returning in the evening, he found Coleridge in the same place, the button in his hand, and, as to the argument, the seemingly hopeless antagonists of the morning, metaphysics and science, religion and science, the two together, or metaphysics religion and science all three, completely reconciled ([6]).

It is of course a misstatement to speak of seeing opposing views or principles reconciled, if one has not followed the process by which the reconciliation has been effected. But we have a phase of general affinity with the imperfection, an excuse for speaking thus, in the circumstance that with individuals who have quarrelled, their manner alone can show us that they are reconciled, without our knowing how the reconciliation was brought about.

This phase of general affinity is only needed when we take the sentence in the anecdote in the strict sense of personal assurance of the reconciliation; for if we regard the words in a colloquial or idiomatic sense, they mean no more than that Lamb finds that Coleridge considers he has completely cleared away the difficulties; a wholly sensible statement.

The verbal mistake is sometimes made, but perhaps more often merely entered upon, and perceived and arrested before complete, of conveying the opposite idea to what is intended by presenting the words necessary for the intended idea in a wrong order, but one which closely resembles the right one, and is, moreover, a grammatical arrangement of words. Probably a not uncommon occasion of a mistake of this kind is where the respective parts of a compound sentence contain two possessive pronouns the substantives belonging to which are diametrically opposed; the mistake lying in transposing the two pronouns, through a confusion made possible (while it requires a circumstance of "general affinity" to make it wholly natural) by the general grammatical connection which each possesses with the substantive belonging, on the particular occasion, to the other one. Thus, taking an illustration from a novel called *The Heir Expectant*, a person addressing the legatee of a deceased uncle, has the intention of saying, "What has been your loss" (the presumably lamented death, though the uncle was eighty-seven, and no very amiable character) "is his gain" (in the shape of spiritual welfare). While his actual words are—what indeed, if the sentence begun had been completed, is an unquestionable truth in one direction at least—" What is his loss is your" (⁷)—' gain,' he is about to say, but corrects himself; " What has been your loss has been his gain, I mean." The originally intended sentence is of course a circumstance of close affinity with the half-uttered erroneous expression.

Indication of temporary ignorance of the name of an intimate friend, with whom, moreover, one is actually in the course of conversation at the time, is, of course, an extreme degree of imperfection. Such an imperfection is commonly shown only when one's attention is totally abstracted from the circumstances of the moment, and the indication of ignorance consequently made mechanically. There is then not what can be called an excuse for the imperfection, but a special cause for it, in the total absence of mind. There are, however, times when this imperfection may be naturally exhibited without complete abstraction, viz., occasions when there is a partial absence of mind, and some circumstance arises giving an excuse for the error, whence the imperfection has circumstantial novelty. Samuel Rogers, the banker and poet, had mentioned to a very absent-minded friend of his—a Mr. Maltby—that at a recent party a lady had come up to him and asked him if his name was not Rogers. " And was it ? " said the other ([8]). The excuse here seems to be that since usually one must be ignorant of a large proportion of all communications made by another person to a third party in one's absence, a permanent fact, such as a name, might be instinctively regarded as one of the former items of information by a person giving only a divided attention to the matter.

The imperfections which present an appearance only of being wholly natural of production consist mainly, it would seem, of expectations of events contrary to the plainest principles of human procedure, and professions of belief in occurrences contrary to the laws of Nature as known to us, the excuse being the first of the two descriptions. We have an instance of the former category of imperfections in a remark made by, I think,

Prince Metternich, to his wife:—"I notice that your bonnets as you buy them gradually get smaller and smaller, and the bills get larger and larger. Some day, I expect, the man will bring nothing but the bill" ([9]). It is the gradual diminution in the size of the bonnets without diminution in the amount of the bills which forms an excuse for the expectation that a man will ask for a payment without having any rational grounds for claiming it; as also—for the imperfection extends in idea to the milliner—for an expectation by the latter of receiving payment under such circumstances. Illustrations from the other category, viz., of professions of belief in occurrences contrary to the laws of Nature, are found in two items of what is commonly known as American humour; the assertion in regard to some tree that it was so high that it took two men and a boy to see to the top of it ([10]), and again of a piece of wood that it was painted so like marble that it sank in the water ([11]). The excuse for the first belief is that ability or performance in many respects increases in proportion to the numbers engaged in a proceeding; and that for the second, the endowment of a piece of wood to a very considerable extent with the attributes of marble, whence to ascribe to it a further quality of marble which it cannot possess, viz., that of great weight, has an appearance of being quite natural.

## CIRCUMSTANTIAL NOVELTY No. 1.

Passing to the second description of excuse—the fact that the imperfection is the result of procedure which under ordinary circumstances would involve no imperfection, or but an inconsiderable degree of it; we have instances ([12], [13]) of the former category in incidents Nos. 1 and 2, Chap. VI., Pt. II. Ordinarily a speech unobjectionable in itself would be followed by no undesirable consequences, but in these speeches discourtesy is involved.

It is to be observed that it is not this discourtesy which is the imperfection excused, for the speaker is not aware at the time of producing his utterance of having exhibited any phase at all in the shape of an offensive sequence to his speech. The imperfection in a measure exercised is the error of judgment (adventitions inferiority; Sect. I., Class II. of imperfections) in concluding for a time, viz., till the speech has been made, that the words are innocuous.

Discourtesy, as is shown in Chapters IV. and VIII. (Sect. VI.), is one of those phases (of which there are not more than two or three descriptions in all) which are at once risible and the reverse of risible in the exhibitor; risible in virtue of loss of dignity, and the reverse of risible in virtue of being an offence to another.

An incident from the other category is seen in a schoolboy's conclusion, after a sum in arithmetic, that several million yards of wall paper would be required for an ordinary sized room ([14]). As to the excuse, a large number of sums done as a process of education are dissociated from the affairs of practical life, whence a mistake is the imperfection of an excess or deficiency of figures solely, an imperfection which is compatible with common sense, and procedure which cannot have the principles of common sense applied to it as a test of approximate correctness. This naturally tends to the omission of the test of common sense when that can be applied.

The second and smaller class of circumstantial novelty No. 1 is composed of risible phases in the shape of want of discrimination or perception, from bringing one's defects, risible or moral, into special prominence, such prominence having a fully natural cause in the presence of a substantial excuse. There are, it seems to me, two divisions of this class, the first composed of incidents where, the magnitude of a risible imperfection in another being the measure of a risible imperfection in oneself, such magnitude of imperfection in the other is expatiated upon, and one's own imperfection thus voluntarily emphasized; showing the further imperfection, viz., want of perception, which I am now concerned with. The second division is formed of incidents where, superiority in oneself in one direction being the measure of one's inferiority, risible or moral, in another direction, such superiority is likewise brought into special prominence, with the result of directing attention to one's inferiority, and thus exhibiting the want of perception.

We should have an illustration of the first division if one of the staff of a newspaper, having in the regular editor's absence written and inserted a libellous article, were to descant on a storm of abuse (imperfection of Sect. VI., Class I.; loss of the natural intellectual dignity of man) which came from the editor on discovering what had been done [15]. In producing the libellous article the writer has shown want of caution (imperfection of Sect. I., Class II.), and since the magnitude of the invective shows the measure of the writer's imperfection, the latter is emphasized in proportion as the invective is descanted on.

Of the second division instances are given of want of perception from emphasizing risible and moral infirmities respectively, one of each. The first is Mrs. Gamp's reply to Betsey Prig, in *Martin Chuzzlewit*, when at the celebrated tea drinking Mrs. Prig asks the other if she knows whom she is speaking to: "Aperiently to Betsey Prig. Aperiently so" [16]. The word "aperiently" is a risible imperfection in the shape of defective pronunciation, repeated, and thus brought into special prominence, presumably because—this forming the excuse for the repetition—of its graceful rhythm, or if not for that reason, at any rate because it is a more or less imposing word.

An instance of one's giving special prominence to a moral inferiority in himself is seen in a passage from *Cecil's Tryst*, by Mr. James Payn, where the manager of a transpontine theatre plumes himself, in the presence of the author, on being able to bring out a play by him with (an emergency having arisen) no more than one day available for rehearsal; not seeing that much in the same proportion to the scantiness of rehearsal is injustice done by him to the author's reputation. "Not one of my company," said Mr. Bingles, in triumph (addressing the author himself on the day of performance) "knew a line of it yesterday morning" ([17]).

## CHAPTER VIII.

### DETAILED ILLUSTRATION OF RISIBLE PHASES (CLASS I.).

I HAVE now to show by detailed illustration, in this and the next two chapters, the several forms of risible imperfection, in the three general phases of retrogression, experience of obstruction of legitimate progress, and inferiority (not being moral).

The first Section of Class I. comprises, as stated, imperfection as follows:—Diminution, depreciation in value, or total loss (by such means as obviously give no return or prospect of return in value) of valuable property owned; or evidence of the possession of an expectation or of a prospect of such diminution, depreciation, or loss. Imperfections of this kind, when the property is of a material description, are caused by such means as forcible deprivation, threats, the operation of inanimate Nature, or our own inadvertence solely. When loss of material property is accompanied by no feature of interest, the appeal to the risible faculties made by the incident would not be of any substantial force, but merely of a mechanical nature. But even this appeal would be overpowered by the feeling of sympathy (inconsiderable, of course, when the loss is trivial, but still existent) or, where sympathy is absent, by the sense that it is called for by the loss, making it unseemly for one to smile. When interest attaches to the loss (not being individual interest from some personal animosity) it lies in the presence of an imperfection in another direction, more or less noticeable, or of ingenuity (first species) in effecting the deprivation, or of both combined. We have an incident showing the combination of imperfection (in the shape of mental inferiority) of a moderately noticeable degree, and ingenuity, in the well-known "confidence trick," by which two confederates delude an inexperienced person into parting with his money, one confederate professing to be unknown to the other and trusting him out of his sight with money, which the other duly returns to repay, the dupe being then induced to do the like with his money, when the recipient, of course, absconds ([1]). Here, in addition to the loss of money, there is inferiority in the matter of acquirement of experience of the world, and ingenuity—that of the original inventor of the trick. In these cases where there are incidental features of interest in themselves, these necessarily attract some attention, even though we may sympathise with the loser. While if the loss is quite inappreciable, the occasion is one on which unalloyed pleasure may be taken.

Expenditure of energy, mental or physical, without a corresponding or any return, one form of which expenditure is shown when one is startled, would come under the category of loss of material property.

Deprivation of valuable property made in punishment for injustice or for non-fulfilment of duty would, as I have before mentioned, be excluded from the category of risible imperfections as being counterbalanced by previous gain from the injustice.

The immaterial property, the forfeiture, deprivation, loss, or absence of which indicates imperfection, is such as expectations, and prospects, *i.e.*, appreciable chances, of substantial property of value; esteem stated to be withheld in consequence of alleged moral inferiority which it is plain to all but the accuser, and to him too in the case of accusations not intended to be believed in, does not exist (producing humour because there has been no injustice to give a counterbalancing gain); and one or more of our own faculties, for a time or permanently.

The expectations of substantial property of value, the destruction of which expectations causes risible imperfection, would be those created by promises of free gifts. It is, of course, non-fulfilment, or intimation of the withdrawal, of the promise which effects a destruction of the expectation.

The prospects, *i.e.*, appreciable chances of such gifts are another form of immaterial property, and the withdrawal of the promise of the gift, whether intimated or not to the former possessor of the chance, destroys the possession.

The intimation of disbelief in any statement which seems false also destroys a substantial, that is, appreciable expectation—real, or, if the discredited statement seems a jocular falsehood, ostensible only—of belief in the statement, and the prospect or chance of such belief. But this destruction of expectation and chance, or destruction of chance only if the presenter of the statement is not told that he is disbelieved (thus, while losing his chance, possessing an expectation, of indefinite degree of strength) has no appearance of a risible imperfection, because such loss, losses, or prevention of gain as might be occasioned by the disbelief expressed or unexpressed, would have the appearance of no retrogression, nor

## RISIBLE PHASES (CLASS I.). 183

of legitimate progress obstructed, but of deprivation of apparently unjust gain, or obstruction of apparently unjust progress. (When the statement, while seeming false, is true, there is a risible imperfection existent, but not exhibited; belonging to Sect. III. of this Class—experience of obstruction, by the disbelief, of legitimate progress: this imperfection can only become apparent by proof being given of the statement being true, upon which proof the imperfection ceases. So long, therefore, as a true statement seems false, there is no appearance of risible imperfection—though it exists unexhibited, in the shape of this obstruction. This same risible imperfection in the shape of obstruction of legitimate progress is of course exhibited, as well as existent, when a discredited statement not only is but seems true.)

The destruction, then, of an apparent substantial expectation, real or ostensible only, of success of what seems an attempt, serious or jocular, at deceit, or the destruction of the chance only, does not, as such a destruction, cause any appearance of risible imperfection in the loser. But inasmuch as he exhibits an error of judgment—real, if the attempt is serious, and ostensible only, if it is jocular—in entertaining a substantial expectation of credence (this error being what I call an incidental inferiority) and also exhibits a further and necessarily real error of judgment (adventitious inferiority) in concluding, as he necessarily must, that there is some chance, though not substantial, of credence, he exhibits imperfections which are risible. These risible imperfections are also exhibited when a real disbelief in a statement which there is no good reason for discrediting is intimated. They come under Sect. I., Class II., and will be found there referred to.

Intimations of the withdrawal of esteem in consequence of alleged moral inferiority which it is obvious to others does not exist, may be made under conditions of two kinds; the first, when the circumstances are such as to leave no reasonable doubt that the intimation is jocular, *i.e.*, not intended to be believed as a true indication of the opinion of the speaker; and the second, when the intimation is made for another purpose than jocularity, upon grounds which do not appear to others reasonable enough to warrant any suspicion of the alleged inferiority, and indeed may be of the most transparently invalid nature.

Of the jocular deprivations of esteem, we have instances in the application of the terms scoundrel, villain, etc., for offences which are at once trivial and unintentional.

Of deprivation for other purposes than jocularity we should have an instance where a person making an obviously inoffensive remark is accused by another, in for instance the familiar meta-

# RISIBLE PHASES (CLASS I.).

phorical language of putting the finger in the pie, of exceeding his or her rights in making the speech.

Time is, of course, a property of value as a means for the acquisition of other things. To procure, by falsehood or other means, the occupation of this, accompanied by more or less expenditure of energy—further valuable property—in a useless manner, is with children a common form of joke, coming under this category of loss of valuable property without return. Getting one to listen to worthless or superfluous information is one variety of this kind of jocularity. One's own judgment, uninfluenced by any intention in others to mislead, may also produce the like result. Where, as is the case in some incidents of the two lastly mentioned descriptions, unprofitable expenditure of time is due to mental inferiority in the loser of the time—imperfection of Sect. I., Class II.—then, although imperfection of the present class and section is shown, it is a subordinate and inappreciable feature of the incident, the mental inferiority being the prominent feature.

Interruption by speech or movement produces this waste of time, and may be done either as a practical joke or seriously for other objects.

Section II.—Possession of property giving pain, or evidence of an expectation or of a prospect of this, without compensation in some form. No illustrations, I think, of this form of imperfection are needed. Here, as with previously mentioned incidents, where the issues are at all serious the appeal to the feeling of sympathy precludes laughter; and it is chiefly in humorous fiction only that pain, substantial or in prospect, can with propriety be referred to jocularly. As regards pain given as punishment for moral inferiority, the gain from the offence would, as with punishment by deprivation of valuable property, be excluded from the category of risible imperfection, from implying a counterbalancing gain from the offence, though as punishment may at times be in excessive proportion to the offence, a general principle of equivalents may be contradicted to any extent by the actual events.

Section III.—Experience of obstruction of legitimate progress. This of course also involves imperfection of Sect. I., in the shape of loss, for a greater or less period, of time, energy, and it may be, money, without even a bare equivalent in return; but it may, I presume, be said that the appearance of the latter imperfection is merged in the more comprehensive one of obstruction of progress. The following are perhaps the only forms of this imperfection which need description or mention. Dishonest falsehood, as stated in Chapter IV., causes, from its implying the withholding of valuable information, imperfection of this description, except, that is, where the information desired would serve the purpose of redress of previous injustice, when the result of a falsehood as regards risibility is the continuance of the imperfection caused by the injustice, instead of the statement tending, as it would if it were true, to the termination of the imperfection.

An intimation of disbelief, real or professed only, in a true statement, causes in the presenter of the statement, provided he has not through previous dishonesty lost his ordinary right to be believed, an obstruction of legitimate progress, exhibited to such as know or believe the statement to be true.

Speaking first of genuine disbelief in a true statement, the progress obstructed would be of indefinite degree, varying according to the circumstances of the case. Where the object of the statement was some practical benefit, the progress obstructed would vary, according to circumstances, from the full amount of such benefit to a fraction thereof, of any minuteness. If the owner of a park who was willing to let persons into it provided the grounds were not injured by them, were, from disbelieving the assurance of care given by a trustworthy applicant, to refuse admission to him, the full benefit sought by the latter would be lost in consequence. If a commission to execute a contract depended on belief in a statement, and no other profitable employment of his time was to be found by the applicant for the contract, the loss would be such profit as was likely to accrue from the undertaking sought. If other directions of work were open to the applicant, the progress lost would be only that of profitable remuneration for his time, and—if it were to be used in the execution of the work and lay uninvested—employment of his capital, for the period of the negotiations with the person having the contract for disposal. While where the result of belief in a statement would be that a person would gratuitously use his interest to obtain a contract for the other, the loss would not be that of the estimated profit from the contract, but what the interest to be exerted was worth to the other. In a case where there is no question of deceit, but a statement is discredited, as where an item of news is supposed to be and is given as authentic, but is not believed, there would be, I should say, a loss of the pleasure which I presume one may be said to feel in the acceptance as true of a true item of news communicated by him.

As regards disbelief in a piece of news, which —the disbelief—is professed but not real (a form of falsehood);—where the falsity of the intimation of disbelief is not perceived by the other he loses, till enlightened, the pleasure just previously mentioned. If the intimation is given under circumstances allowing no reasonable doubt of the falsity of the profession (as where the person professing disbelief is joking and his tone or other circumstances point to this) this pleasure would, of course, not be lost, but at the same time in virtue of the intimation of disbelief there is an ostensible, while not real, loss of such pleasure by him.

Where a piece of news is false, and is refused credence, there would still be an exhibition (delusive) of obstruction of legitimate progress to any person who believed the statement to be true.

In the incident No. 21, Chapter VI., Part I., we have, as before, obstruction through discredit of one's speech, with the difference, however, that the speech is not an individual statement, but a person's conversation in general. "The house, emptied of so much, is full of echoes, and its owner's voice returns to him without contradiction;" that is, he receives after an utterance a return of his own words instead of a contradiction ($^2$). The obstruction (not stated in words, but indicated by inference) caused by the systematic contradiction Paterfamilias meets with when the family are at home, is that of the general progress resulting from the acceptance of one's speech as correct; such progress being legitimate because a substantial proportion, at least, of credence to his utterances is the right of every average individual.

The pertinence, or *raison d'être*, of describing the head of a family as meeting with constant contradiction at home, probably lies in the circumstance that in real life the head of a family, while not receiving more contradiction at home than the other members, yet, being presumably entitled to a special measure of deference, often receives less of this than he ought to.

Another form of this imperfection, varying from a trivial degree upwards, is caused when a person speaking is interrupted by another utterance made under the impression, or ostensible impression, that the last speaker has anticipated the other's ideas. The imperfection is shown in its slightest degree when the obstructor is at once interrupted with the remark that he has not apprehended the other correctly, and thereon allows him to proceed. The loss here would be that of the net benefit, *i.e.*, the benefit after deducting the value of one's time and trouble, resulting from the expression of thought, to the other's comprehension, in respect of the period occupied by the explanation of the true state of the matter—the explanation that the obstructionist had misapprehended one. On other occasions the obstruction may be greater, and need to remove it two persons speaking at once for an objectionable length of time, or the drowning of the other's voice if he is specially intent on his own course.

Section IV.—Evidence of absence of some special property or benefits common to the generality, or evidence of ownership of such property of less extent or of less value than that owned by the generality. The assertion made by Talleyrand, that the English had a thousand religions and only one sauce ([3]), is an instance of the latter form of humour; and if we alter the remark to the extent of denying the possession of any sauce to our nation ([4]), it will serve as an illustration of the other form of imperfection. Here the generality is not one of individuals, but of nations.

Section V.—A less favourable situation than that of the generality in respect of environment or external advantages. In the *Songs of Singularity*, by the London Hermit, there are the lines —

> "He stood on his head by the lone sea shore,
> And joy was the cause of the act;
> For he felt as he never had felt before,
> Insanely glad, in fact.
>
> "And why ? In that ship that had left the bay,
> His mother-in-law had sailed
> To a tropical country far away,
> Where tigers and snakes prevailed "([5]).

In this proximity of tigers and snakes there is a less favourable environment for the lady in respect of animals than pertains to the inhabitants of this country, whose condition, as that ordinarily coming under one's observation, would form the standard to which he would refer the condition of an inhabitant of another country. The dandy of one of the comic papers, at a time when very tight trousers were in fashion, who is represented as saying to a friend that he could not sit down at the time because he had on his walking trousers ([6]), gives another instance of this humour, the extra tight clothes constituting an unfavourable environment from depriving him of the ability, common to the generality, of sitting down at any time. There would further be mental inferiority in the want of common sense shown in the choice of such a costume, as also, perhaps, of such approximations to it as may have been worn by the dandies of real life.

An imperfection of this section is in fact the sum of imperfections in the form of loss, pain, etc.—classed under previous sections—which are caused by the unfavourable situation; these lesser imperfections being such as painful prospects, expenditure of extraordinary time and trouble in securing safety where loss of that is threatened, and in precluding annoyance in various ways from the situation. Since, however, in contemplating one of these general situations we do not resolve it into the various individual imperfections involved or likely to be involved in the situation, but regard it as indicating a general condition of inferiority, I have thought that a separate section should be made of these cases.

The sixth section relates to loss of dignity. The more ordinary modes in which this is shown would seem to be the physical, the more especially intellectual, and the æsthetic.*

Enumerating these modes more particularly, we find them caused (1) by proceedings unsuited to the physical conformation of the individual; (2) by the more especially intellectual imperfections which constitute violations of class distinctions, distinctions created by the differences in man's occupations at different times and in different places (differences of time and place), those created by differences of age, and descents from the natural intellectual dignity of man; and (3) by descents from the æsthetic degree of perfection appropriate to the individual, shown by lapses, avoidable or unavoidable, from the standard proper to one's class in respect of personal adornment (slovenliness of dress and accidental dilapidation in that respect), and in respect of preservation of natural advantages of personal

* Loss of dignity in the physical and æsthetic directions implies, where it is voluntary, a loss of intellectual dignity; but since such small prominence as the latter would have in itself is merged in that of the physical or æsthetic loss, the imperfections would seem to be appropriately described in the above manner.

appearance (inattention to, or accidental deterioration of, the appearance of the skin by not preserving cleanliness).

Certain exceptional directions in which loss of dignity may be shown, and the loss of dignity involved in dishonour, in its general and in its petty phases, will be referred to separately.

The imperfection caused by a loss of dignity would seem to be (except as regards lack of moral dignity) of a twofold description, being composed of primary and secondary imperfections, as I should call them.

With loss of dignity in the intellectual\* (which includes the social) and æsthetic divisions, the primary imperfection is the loss of the superiority of benefit resulting from procedure or appearance appropriate to a particular class or station, or to an occasion of some gravity and importance, over that resulting from procedure or appearance appropriate only to a lower class or station, or a less serious occasion.

In undignified bodily movements, such as standing on the head, turning somersaults, etc., the primary imperfection lies in various directions. It would take such forms as loss of time on account of the inability for the physical actions, such as walking and ordinary manual labour,

---

\* *I.e.*, the more especially intellectual.

## RISIBLE PHASES (CLASS I.).

which normally procure man his livelihood, the greater or less loss of benefit from the sense of sight (both imperfections of Sect. I., Class I.), the inability to protect himself from collision with any approaching objects (a temporary physical inferiority, and belonging to Sect. I., Class II.), while there should perhaps be added more or less loss of command of the thinking faculties, and the possibility of some measure of physical injury from the unnatural positions. Further, there would be æsthetic inferiority from want of grace in the attitudes. It is probably this latter inferiority which contributes most to the forcible aspect which loss of physical dignity presents, though perhaps the sum total of the other imperfections would at the same time present a very prominent appearance. Grimaces, I should say, are a form of undignified procedure involving imperfection in a physical as well as æsthetic direction, the physical imperfection being expenditure of energy to no purpose ordinarily.

The secondary imperfection in loss of dignity is the loss of esteem of the observer which results from the proceeding, a loss which has a prominence not shown by other imperfections, for the following reason, viz., that the principles determining dignified procedure are distinguished by presenting a broad and general character, making a correct apprehension of them necessarily a possession of everyone having ordinary experience. *Intimations* of loss of esteem cause a definite exhibition of imperfection whatever the defect or alleged defect on account of which the esteem is withdrawn may be, but this of course is by reason of the intimation—the formal evidence of the loss of esteem which it constitutes.

Very little illustration of the ordinary forms of loss of dignity, in addition to what I have already given incidentally, seems required. Instances of violations of class distinctions, and of those created by differences of age, need not, I think, be given. Of procedure undignified by reason of the character of the occasion on which it is exhibited, we have illustrations in jocularity on especially grave occasions—a violation of distinction of time; and in the performance in the midst of business conducted more especially by brain work, of any of the ordinary muscular operations which are ends, not means; this being a violation of distinction of place. Loss of the natural intellectual dignity of man is seen in invective, in the shape of cursing, abuse, etc. Of the third division of undignified phases—descents from æsthetic propriety, I have already mentioned one description, viz., grimaces, which will I think be enough.

A formally recognized position of elevation above the generality—a post of eminence—

implies mental superiority in the holder. And thus any exhibition by him of less dignity than would ordinarily be shown by the generality would involve the additional imperfection of incongruous juxtaposition, an imperfection which would have an especially forcible aspect when the loss of dignity is shown in physical procedure. Hence the effect which the undignified conduct in judges and other high officials, so often seen in burlesques, produces.

Passing to the exceptional directions in which the imperfection may be shown;—On special occasions and in special places, such as Sundays, times of festivity, and exceptionally fashionable resorts, one may hold a higher position in regard to personal adornment and preservation of natural advantages of personal appearance, than in ordinary, from dressing better than usual, and preserving exceptional cleanliness, as we may on these occasions. Hence occurrences—a smut on the face, for instance—which on ordinary occasions would involve a slight, but not more than a slight, loss of dignity, will make the loss greater on these special occasions, from the higher position of the individual then. Mr. H. C. Pennell, in *Puck on Pegasus*, gives an illustration of this in the lines:—

> " I never did the swell
> In Regent Street among the beaux,
> But smuts the most prodigious fell,
> And always settled on my nose " [7].

A person mingling with his social superiors as an equal, concealing his true position, experiences loss of the dignity he has assumed if his true position becomes revealed. The jackdaw of the fable, stripped of his borrowed plumes, is—substituting birds for persons—an illustration of this loss of dignity([8]). In a certain comic song an oil and colour merchant, who, after amassing a fortune, had gained an entrance into the best society, conceals his occupation, till one day a fellow-tradesman rushes up to him in the midst of his fashionable acquaintances, with the loud and effusive inquiry—the first, of course, to be made in humorous fiction under such circumstances, as it would be the last in real life—" How's business? What's the price of oils?"([9])

In dishonourable procedure, as I have mentioned in Chapter IV., there is, in addition to the non-risible imperfection which the injustice of the proceeding constitutes, a risible imperfection—lack of the moral dignity of man, causing the withdrawal of esteem by the observer which forms one of the phases of contempt.

Loss of intellectual dignity is shown in the commission of injustice, by way of dishonour or otherwise, when the nature of the offence from the intellectual point of view is below that proper to the status of the individual. Such actions are treated in their moral bearings on their own demerits in that direction, and the humour of the intellectual inferiority remains distinct, though, of course, the seriousness of the moral aspect divides our attention more or less with the risible side of the matter.

A gentleman practising theft on a petty scale, by the abstraction of any small sum of money or article of trifling value accessible to him ([10]), or any adult making raids upon the store-room for immediate consumption, after the fashion of a child ([11]), shows loss of dignity in this direction.

These proceedings, necessarily acts of injustice, would also, of course, be acts of dishonour if the offenders had had trust placed in them in regard to these matters.

It is said of Queen Elizabeth that the visits she paid to some of her nobles were made with the especial object of lessening their too great power, entailing, as the visits would, heavy expenses on them ([12]). This shows dishonour on a petty scale—as would be all want of honour in matters of social intercourse—the nobles presumably not being bound, except by the voluntarily imposed rules of courtesy, to incur these expenses of hospitality. The lack of dignity, of course, does not exist if the Queen had no such intention in making these visits, but the idea of the imperfection, a striking one, from its magnitude and character as being of systematic presentation, remains.

There is ingenuity of the first species shown if the Queen had this object in view.

The several varieties of discourtesy are perhaps the commonest forms of dishonour on a petty scale.

But little illustration is needed of these offences.

Of the commoner forms of discourteous actions one or two instances have been incidentally given in Chapter IV.

Wilful violations of etiquette are, of course, discourteous, assuming the custom ordained to be a reasonable one.

The unnecessary communication to others, that is, the communication from other motives than the interests of morality, of truths or supposed truths which would be unpleasant to them—procedure involving discourtesy — I have already spoken of in Chapter IV. Where intimations of this kind are intentionally made, and we think the other desires to injure, or is indifferent to our feelings, the moral aspect of the case—the resentment of the offence—would usually overpower the risibility in the loss of dignity. But where an unpleasant truth is presented to one, either (1) jocularly, being then unpleasant rather in form than in substance (2) from the speaker's ignorance at the moment of what the words indicated, by reason of an inference which they bear being not obvious, or (3) from an erroneous impression in him that the person he referred to was not present, the moral aspect of the matter substantially disappears (while remaining, however, in form) as regards the two first descriptions of offences, and in the third is less serious than it would otherwise have been; the thirdly mentioned offence being, I should say, taken out of the category of undignified procedure, and remaining merely an imputation, true or false, of inferiority of the other to the average individual in the matter referred to.

Incidents Nos. 1 and 2, Chapter VI., Part II., give two illustrations ([13, 14]) of the second of these three descriptions of discourtesy, and instances of the other two are not, I think, necessary.

As regards speech discourteous from its tone, or from being wanting in the customary phrases of civility, I have endeavoured in Chapter IV. to state the import of this phraseology and tone, and the risible imperfection which speech lacking in it produces in the person addressed; and no further reference to the subject seems needed.

There is, besides lack of moral dignity in the dishonour itself, loss of moral dignity in any voluntary exhibition of dishonour, not as an act of repentance but because the exposure is necessary to the attainment of some benefit outweighing the loss from the risible imperfection. In Miss Mitford's *Life and Letters*, Basil Montague is recorded as saying, in reference to Dr. Parr's illegible manuscript, "Aye, his letters are illegible, unless they contain a commission or an announcement that he is coming to see you, and then no man can write plainer" ([15]).

The dishonourable element here is discourtesy in writing badly when one can write more legibly —dishonourable because the average individual, who writes legibly, does not give the bad writer the trouble in deciphering which the latter gives him. Dr. Parr, however, practises the discourtesy on a noticeably larger scale than those who, being able to write legibly, write badly on all occasions; for they, although gaining on the whole more than they lose by careless writing, yet, when clear writing is of extra importance to them, as on such occasions as the above, write as usual, and take the risk. Of course, where the bad writer may be considered as compensating the average, *i.e.*, the legible writer, in any way, direct or indirect, for his trouble in deciphering the bad caligraphy, there is no discourtesy exercised.

The voluntary exhibition of dishonour by Dr.

Parr—the lack of moral dignity which the anecdote is quoted to illustrate—is of course in the revelation of the ability to write well.

A very definite proportion of the interest this incident has for us is due, no doubt, to the existence of these occasional conditions making legible writing of special importance, which compel the defaulter to disclose his dishonourable practice under penalty of losing these substantial benefits.

In his history of Frederick the Great of Prussia, Carlyle relates that at the beginning of Frederick's invasion of Silesia, the Burgomaster of Grunberg, on being summoned to deliver the key of the Town Gate for the transit of a Prussian army, says, "Deliver the key! I dare not. There is the key lying, but to *give* it! You are not the Queen of Hungary's officer, I doubt." The Prussian officer then takes the key. A like process happens when the army pass out of the town next day. The Burgomaster will not touch the key, but it may be put back ([16]). This, too, shows loss of moral dignity, in the Burgomaster's voluntary exhibition —unavoidable of course if he is to effect his main object—of his intention to delude his sovereign into supposing, upon the strength of the statement that the key had not been given up, that all available force had been used to bar the army's passage through the town.

This incident presents the additional element of ingenuity of the first species.

Section VII.—Appropriation of articles of utility to other than their ordinary purposes. All appropriation of articles, whether natural products or of human manufacture, to other than their ordinary use, it appears to me constitutes, by reason of man's being normally interested in their appropriation to their ordinary use, exhibition of imperfection on the part, not of any particular individual, but of mankind in general; the form of imperfection being that of depreciation of the value of the property from the fact that while it is thus misused it cannot be applied to its ordinary use. While in so far as the articles may be unfitted for the exceptional use they are put to, it seems to me there would be further imperfection on the part of the person using them of the form mentioned in Sect. IV. of this Class—possession of property of less value than that owned by the generality. It is true that the proper article for the purpose here in view might be one such as many persons would not be in possession of, but this is because the purpose for which it is suited is not one which they have in view. Where the purpose is entertained, a person is normally in possession of the proper article for it. The term generality, therefore, here means the generality of persons who have such purpose in view, and who would have the particular article suited for effecting it.

To play at bowls with apples or potatoes, to use a long roll of bread or a cucumber as a broadsword, to bowl a plate like a hoop, would present humour of this kind.

# CHAPTER IX.

### DETAILED ILLUSTRATION OF RISIBLE PHASES (CLASS II).

THE second class of imperfection comprises a very large proportion of the risible phases giving appreciable amusement to us. The imperfections composing the first section, we have seen, are—Exhibition in transient or permanent form, that is, by transient or permanent productions, of capabilities, acquirements, or endowments, of an inferior degree; exhibition of the total absence of capabilities, acquirements, or endowments in some direction; and exhibition of absence of any capacity for enjoyment common to the generality.

I take first the mental imperfections which may be called adventitious inferiorities, and which consist mainly in the falsification of the judgment in its various forms. An error of judgment, while always constituting an adventitious inferiority, does not necessarily imply intrinsic inferiority, for where there are no data for forming a correct conclusion the actual course of events may be other than what was indicated by human probabilities. The adventitious inferiority shown by a falsification of judgment is in relation to anyone in possession (whether in virtue of his own ability or otherwise) of the knowledge which would have been required to form a correct conclusion. Thus the cleverest and the dullest person, when in possession of the full bearings of the matter, are on a par in possessing alike this adventitious superiority to the other when he formed his conclusion. The person making the error would not be excluded from the number of those to whom the adventitious inferiority in respect of the mistake might be shown, but would, on becoming aware of the mistake, be in the position of superiority to his former self.

Although this inferiority is always a more or less prominent feature in the incident, the interest in it must be of an uniform and slight degree. When appreciable pleasure is given (of course on intellectual, not moral grounds) on occasions of mistakes of judgment, it comes from other sources, such as a recondite nature in data existing for correctness of judgment; the presentation, as the result of the error, of some imperfection of considerable magnitude of degree; or intrinsic incapability shown in the judgment, that is, the judgment being one that a person of average intelligence would not have formed.

If we except, as being a special form of these

imperfections, the falsification of the instinctive judgment by the recipient formed for the moment or longer on the presentation of an "event of the occasion" having a phase of circumstantial novelty No. 2 specially connected with it, the commonest form in which error of judgment is shown is probably the falsification of conclusions in reference to particular matters and upon which some practical issues depend. Errors of judgment in particular matters not involving material issues are found, on occasion, where the judgment was elicited as a test of mental ability.

Errors of judgment may be regarded as forming two divisions; the first that of cases where there were data accessible for forming correct conclusions, and the second that of cases without such material. The speeches ($^{1,\ 2}$) in incidents 1 and 2, Chap. VI., Part II.—injudicious because involving discourtesy (imperfection of Sect. VI., Class I.) — belong to the first division. The above-mentioned falsifications of instinctive judgments consequent on the presentation of phases of novelty with special connections, also belong to this division; though as the data for correct conclusions are for the moment definitely removed from the ordinary mental range, these errors form a category of their own.

There are some errors of this division which

# RISIBLE PHASES (CLASS II.).

are primarily due to a biassing or other agency, and which, if such agency were absent, would indicate intrinsic inferiority of reasoning capability, but which, with such agency, are taken out of this latter category, and merely present the adventitious inferiority. As there are also errors of this kind belonging to the second division of erroneous judgments, I propose to deal with the whole group together, and will accordingly defer illustrations of such as belong to the first division till I have arrived at the second division.

Mistakes of judgment of the second division are those where there was no material accessible for forming a correct conclusion. These may be subdivided into the categories of cases where there were data accessible indicating a probability in favour of what proves the right course, and those where either there were no such data accessible, or where the probabilities, by which of course we shape our conduct, are falsified by the event.

Of the first subdivision are the errors indicated by such hoaxes — jocular impositions upon another's credulity—as are devised for discovering whether, and it may be how much, intrinsic inferiority of capacity for estimating probabilities exists in another, and a proportion (the rest belonging to division I.) of those errors, primarily due to a biassing or other exceptional agency, which errors without such agency would indicate intrinsic inferiority of reasoning power, but which the exceptional agency takes out of the category of intrinsic inferiorities. Instances of these will be given when I have explained the character of the second subdivision of errors.

To the second subdivision belong the errors from those hoaxes which, without eliciting exhibition of inferior capacity for estimating a probability, induce a person to act upon his erroneous judgment by taking procedure resulting in further humour, such as the fruitless journeys and the block resulting from the Berners Street hoax, which filled that street with persons on every kind of business, who in the name of a tenant of one of the houses had been desired to call there ([3]); and practical jokes of various kinds.

With some hoaxes where the procedure taken in consequence of the error is the main object of the joker, the judgment shown in being deceived will be of an intrinsically inferior character, and thus of course belong to the first subdivision.

Illustrating again the first subdivision;—of jokes which might be made for the sole sake of the adventitious inferiority—though of course unprofitable expenditure of time in giving attention to the joker, and, it may be, time and trouble in ascertaining the truth from others, is a necessary result—we should have an instance where a boy tells a schoolfellow that a holiday has been announced, and the other, calculating the chance of the statement being a hoax quite correctly, yet not being omniscient, recognises it as possibly true.([4])

The following is an instance of a judgment not at the time shown to be erroneous, but expected soon to be shown so, and belonging to the first or second subdivision according to what might be considered the data for a judgment in the matter. One of the chapters in Mortimer Collins' *Vivian Romance* is prefaced by a passage called an extract, and from an old Play, but which I understand is a fragmentary composition ascribed to a complete work as an excuse for its existence, and of Mr. Collins' own invention. Summed up, the passage runs, "Did the fellow call me an old fogey? He shall feel the thrust of an old fogey's rapier"([5]). The judgment formed by the "fellow" may, I take it, be regarded as being not that there is the least rational chance of the other challenging him to a duel, but that if he did he would not be in the least dangerous. Sir Robert, the speaker, thinks this conclusion erroneous, and proposes to prove it so. The adventitious inferiority in the other is not yet shown, but Sir Robert contemplates it by anticipation.

Of cases where the probabilities point to a conclusion in one direction, while the event takes another, we have instances in all those conclusions on occasions of humour by surprise (Chapter VI., Part II.), which are not suspended after the first instant in view of a possible joke; viz., those absolute instinctive permanent conclusions which are formed when there is no suspicion of a joke, and any reasoned conclusions short of the absolute, which recognise the possibility of a joke, but are formed because there are probabilities in favour of the event taking the ordinary direction. Of the more ordinary varieties of this subdivision it is, I think, scarcely necessary to give illustration.

There are, as I have mentioned, certain erroneous judgments, belonging, according to the occasion, to the first or second division, made by individuals, or aggregates of persons, of average reasoning capability, which errors are due to a biassing agency, and which if such agency had not existed would have indicated risible inferiority of reasoning power—inferiority to the average—and thus would not have been made without the bias, except in fiction. Excitement, self-interest, and the influence of custom, may be mentioned as illustrations of biassing agencies in the formation of such judgments. Instances need not be given of errors by persons of average capability which in the absence of excitement, or of self-interest, would not have been made by them. The circumstance that credence may as a rule be given to what is presented in newspapers illustrates the thirdly mentioned biassing agency. Without a biassing element—if, for instance, a statement were presented under conditions which made it equally likely, apart from the character of the statement itself, to be truth or fiction; made, let us say, on a torn piece of paper which might be either from a work of fiction or from a periodical professing to relate real events—a judicious conclusion would be formed by the person of average capability if the conclusion were such as to need no more than that measure of capability. With the bias, however, hoaxes presented in newspapers will occasionally deceive persons of average capability.

The exceptional agencies other than bias which may cause erroneous judgments which would not otherwise be made, are such as forgetfulness, special ignorance, carelessness, absence of mind, and abstraction. The feature which distinguishes these agencies from a bias in connection with an error of judgment is the circumstance that where one of these conditions prevails the whole data for a judgment correct or probably correct are not possible to be seen by the person taking procedure, whereas the presence of bias does not necessarily preclude a proper decision. Thus, to take an illustration from a comic paper, if a person has stowed away some small parcels on his head and under his hat, and forgets the circumstance, it is not possible that he should take steps to avoid places where he may meet lady friends, before whom his hat should be removed ([6]). If one were ignorant that some compound was an expensive drug, and supposed it to be a common phosphate such as bone dust, he could not conclude that it would be injudicious to manure a field with it ([7]). And if abstraction prevented one from thinking definitely what he was saying, he could not conclude it was injudicious to say "Yes" to a question which was injudiciously answered by that word ([8]).

Of course bias or one of these other agencies may cause an error which even without the exceptional agency would not indicate intrinsic inferiority of reasoning power, as where an error which the generality would make under ordinary circumstances and which a person of superior reasoning power would not, is made by the latter, through the presence of an exceptional agency. But since without this agency the error would indicate no intrinsic inferiority of reasoning capacity, the agency does not, as in the other instances, present itself for attention as a factor in the commission of the error, and the only noticeable feature is the adventitious inferiority

## RISIBLE PHASES (CLASS II.). 215

in the error, with any risible imperfection which may result from the conclusion formed.

All belief in falsehood is of course error of judgment, of the first or second subdivision according to whether the probabilities pointed to distrust or belief in the statement. The error of course would not be proved till the falsity of the statement was proved; while for the error to be suspected by third parties it would be requisite that they should themselves discredit the statement and have evidence satisfying them that the other put belief in it.

Procedure taken in consequence of belief in falsehood would usually result in inferiority in the deceived person, of character according to the nature of the procedure, it being of course usually the jocular falsehoods—hoaxes,—which bring about imperfection of magnitude or prominence.

In Sect. I. of Class I. I mentioned that in the destruction, by intimation of disbelief in a statement, of an expectation and chance of success of what seems an attempt, real or ostensible, at deceit, or in the destruction—when the statement is disbelieved but no intimation of disbelief is made to the producer—of the chance alone, there remained two elements of risible imperfection exhibited, belonging to the present class and section, in the shape of errors of judgment; such errors being (1) the conclusion, real, or ostensible only, that there was a substantial, *i.e.*, appreciable, chance of the statement being believed, (such conclusion being an incidental inferiority) and (2) the conclusion, (adventitious inferiority) which must necessarily be real, that there is some chance, even though infinitesimal, of belief in the statement. These are necessary items of imperfection in all unsuccessful attempts at deceit; for although as regards false statements which are not intended to be believed, there is no real expectation of a substantial degree that the attempt will be successful—no real expectation stronger than everyone must entertain till positive disbelief is intimated —there is, I hold, always an ostensible expectation of such substantial degree by reason of the circumstance, which I take for granted, that we presume that under normal circumstances, that is, under the serious aspect of life, according to which all detected departure from truth entails real penalties, no one would risk the penalties of detected deceit unless he thought he had a substantial chance of the falsehood being successful.

These same risible imperfections, as was stated in Sect. I. Class I., are caused where real disbelief in a statement which there is yet no good reason for discrediting is intimated. In these cases, however, there would be no prominence in the errors of judgment (committed of course not in reference to persons in general, but only as regards the particular individual disbelieving without good reason), and only the moral issues would call for consideration.

Besides these necessarily existent items of inferiority, real as regards the adventitious, and real or ostensible only, according to occasion, as regards the incidental, there would be intrinsic inferiority of a real character attributed by any disbeliever in a statement who credited the presenter of it with a degree of real belief in success greater than he considered a person of average sense would entertain.

The other mode in which adventitious inferiority is shown is seen where some commonly received opinion is pronounced incorrect, upon the authority of some person of eminence; the inferiority being shown by those who hold or held the opinion to those who agree with the pronunciation against it. The dicta of the satirist indicate instances of this imperfection, an element of moral inferiority being in the case of satire presented in conjunction with the mental imperfection.

I now arrive at instances of intrinsic inferiority exclusively. First may be mentioned exhibitions of defective common sense, by which term I understand sense of not less than a considerable degree below the average. A large proportion of these inferiorities, as shown in Chapter VI., are exhibitions of defective common sense accompanying the presentation of phases of circumstantial novelty No. 2, and carrying formal presumptive evidence of conscious invention. The following are a few instances of this inferiority not exhibited with phases of circumstantial novelty; all of them being fictitious and some bearing every evidence—not being of the formal description—of the defect being ostensible only.

Particular properties we know are adapted to give pleasure to particular senses. If one fixes the eye upon a turnip he receives no emotion; while he may boil down the finest painting with his leg of mutton without any result that is at all satisfactory ([9]). It is true there would be various opportunities for jokes upon a proceeding of the latter description. A guest might point out to his host that the palette should go to the painting, not the painting to the palate. Another might say that he had always hitherto been accused of a want of taste for the old masters, but that no one could charge him with it now. One might hear from a third: "This was not an old master. I always had my doubts about the genuineness of your Raphael; but there is a modern pungency about this paint that puts the matter beyond all

# RISIBLE PHASES (CLASS II.). 219

question." Whereon the host might glare at a fourth, who had sold him the picture and was himself a painter, and read Nemesis upon his countenance if he was a scholar, conscious guilt and retribution if he was no more than a plain honest man.

Such ignorance of a natural principle as the foregoing indicates a deficiency of common sense. The nausea from the swallowing of paint is imperfection of Sect. II., Class I.

In Miss Braddon's *Sir Jasper's Tenant*, already quoted from elsewhere, Mr. Dobbs says to Dorothy Tursgood, in discussing the details of a proposed picnic, " No, Miss Tursgood, not six pair of fowls, as I see you are thinking of for your contribution; we will only tax you to the extent of a couple " [10]. He is here speculating on Dorothy's intended contribution, and exhibits want of common sense in this ostensible supposition of twelve fowls as her portion, as although she might think of being thus munificent, the common probabilities are that she would contemplate providing neither much more nor much less than an average contribution for one person.

In *A Perilous Secret*, by Charles Reade, we have the words, "That's the advantage he has over me," suggested Walter; "she is five feet eight or thereabouts, so he is just the height of her heart " [11]. Here there is profession of the belief that the correspondence of the total height of the one person—under five feet—with the altitude of the heart of the other, would be likely to endear the two to each other. This physical correspondence forming an excuse for the imperfection, the latter possesses circumstantial novelty No. 1. (class 1).

Attaching undue importance to small matters is a common form of inferiority. Instances are seen in the two following, primarily due, however, the first to an idiosyncrasy, and the second to the bias of self-interest. The first illustration ([12]) is given in the incident No. 20, Chapter VI., Part I.; "Now this old gentleman prided himself on the neatness of his dispatches. A blot on the paper darkened his soul." In one of Edgar Poe's tales a resuscitated mummy is being interrogated on the state of civilization of the ancient Egyptians, with the result of showing their superiority in almost all matters to the moderns, when finally the inquiry is made, compared with which all others are evidently regarded as trivial, "'Did your countrymen comprehend the mode of manufacture of Ponnonner's lozenges?' ([13]) We waited anxiously for the reply, but none came. The mummy hung his head abashed, and was silent. Never was victory more complete; never was defeat borne with so ill a grace. I reached my hat, bowed stiffly, and withdrew." The air of dignified contempt shown in the latter process is in amusing accord with the consciousness of a great intellectual victory on the part of the moderns. This estimate of the relative importance of the lozenges and the general attainments of the Egyptians, shows a want of common sense which probably would be exhibited with serious intent by no one in real life, even allowing for the bias of self-interest. The mummy, in accepting the estimate, of course makes the same exhibition of defective common sense, but without the bias.

The presentation of bad and indifferent wit is a form of mental inferiority in respect of the opinion that it is worth producing. Wit which has for its end some personal object as well as pleasure to the intellectual sense of persons in general, can often claim exemption from the category of bad or indifferent wit, although showing a degree of inventive power too slight to be worth presentation if it could be conceived solely with reference to the pleasure it gives to the intellectual sense of the generality.

Under this Class would come proceedings falling short of the arbitrary standards of correct procedure fixed by convention—non-observances of custom, ceremony, or etiquette. These standards, of course, vary according to the social body, but it is the variations from the standards of the general society of one's country which most prominently bear the appearance of humour.

The ordinances of convention founded on natural principles of propriety, as distinct from its arbitrary ordinances, such as etiquette or fashion, we call civilization, refinement, or culture. Here whole communities may show imperfection.

Of course inferiority both in respect of civilization and etiquette is not mental incapability, but ignorance of special knowledge—inferiority of acquirement. And the term generality, from whose measure of acquirement the procedure is judged, has a less extended application, the degrees of limitation being of all varieties, than where matters of inferior mental capabilities are concerned.

Transcending conventional standards of morality in certain directions—standards approved or admitted by convention, but inadmissible on strict moral principles—is in the eyes of convention a form of intellectual inferiority. The directions in which this excessive observance of moral principles has this appearance of humour would seem to be mainly those where the lower degree of morality would diminish the welfare of others to but little or no appreciable extent, and would at the same time obviate confession of some inferiority, moral or intellectual, in oneself.

An undergraduate at an examination was told by the examiner afterwards that a failure to answer some question was, the latter supposed, due to nervousness. "No, sir, it was ignorance," the other replied ([14]). To let the examiner credit him with a knowledge he was without, would, although even convention might not like to endorse the proceeding with its formal approval, yet be recognised as excusable, seeing that temptation was put in the undergraduate's way—would be all that was positively expected of him; whence to make the confession of ignorance has a certain appearance of intellectual inferiority, as being not positively necessary.

The point of view from which the strict moralist would regard this procedure would, I should say, be as follows. From the standpoint of strict morality, confession of the truth can under no circumstances constitute intellectual inferiority, but even the strict moralist would, probably, from seeing convention regard as unnecessary, confession of such a truth as this, instinctively refer this confession to convention's standard of morality likewise (or if he did not do this, would at least entertain in idea, from familiarity with convention's standpoint, an exhibition of intellectual inferiority). He would thus instinctively (or else in idea) regard the confession as humorous, although his reason (or else his judgment of actual, as distinct from ideal, events) referring the confession to the higher standpoint of strict morality, recognises the confession as involving no intellectual inferiority.

Superfluous, unnecessary observances in the general phases of procedure to which courtesy belongs, indicate mental inferiority. In Anthony Trollope's *Doctor Thorne*, the doctor, who had newly furnished his house for the reception of his adopted daughter, Mary, jocularly tells the child that he should never dare to come into the drawing-room without her permission, and not then till he had taken off his boots [15].

As regards manual arts, useful and ornamental, these for the most part pertain to some one or other of the several special walks of life, in which the generality are not engaged, and inferiority in which forms the material of Sect. IV. of this Class. Some few are practised by the generality, and of these writing is probably the foremost.

Caricatures present æsthetic defects, indicating also physical imperfection in other respects according to the feature or features exaggerated, altered, or omitted. A head of enormous size implies an extra expenditure of energy to support it, without compensation for such expenditure.

Inability to perceive the humour in a risible situation is, of course, a mental inferiority. We have an instance [16] in the last words in the following passage, which begins, it will be observed, by a transfer to the subject of twins of the general form of words in which runs the well-known saying on greatness, "Some persons are born twins, some achieve them, and others have twins thrust upon them. It would be an interesting matter for consideration whether the honours of twinship might not, to some extent, at any rate, be accorded to members of a family who, while not entering the world at the same time, voluntarily went out of it together, when it would be said of them, They were not born twins, but they have done what they could."

The distinction, such as it is, in twinship, lies in twin births being intrinsically rare events, which is in no wise the case with a simultaneous exit from the world of members of a family, however rare of occurrence the latter event may be. There is, however, a superficial appearance of the two events being, after making exception of their belonging to opposite periods of life, of precisely the same description: in fact, the simultaneous exit is a circumstance of general affinity with the condition of genuine twinship which forms an excuse for the supposition that the former proceeding would be a substantially equivalent condition to twinship of birth, and consequently makes this supposition a phase of circumstantial novelty No. 1. (class I.). To this imperfection is, of course, added the further one of surrendering life for the purpose of gaining the very qualified distinction of twinship. In the comment furnishing my illustration,—" They were not born twins," etc.—not only is the imperfection in the would-be twins unperceived, but even terms of approval are applied to their act.

Nonsense may be defined as a grammatically constructed sentence presenting a combination of ideas which is inconceivable to the mind either by reason of the sentence in itself or by reason of circumstances under which it is presented. Of the former division are such statements as that the sun and moon are identical, that a particular object appears to a particular person at a given time wholly rough and wholly smooth, or that it appears at that moment wholly white and wholly black. Of the second division would be the statement to a person who has the speaker in view at the time, that the latter is touching some article, when really separate from it. Here the evidence of the other's eyes makes the statement inconceivable to him. To say that one believes inanimate objects have reasoning powers is an inconceivable proposition, for the word inanimate indicates exclusion of all powers of thought.

Although a nonsensical proposition is on the whole inconceivable, it will present by suggestion a conceivable situation—which I should term an approximate one—in virtue of the ideas combined in the sentence being conceivable, the character of which situation would be determined by the nature of the ideas combined, while on the subjective side it would often be variously apprehended according to the particular person to whom it is presented. Thus if a person inside a house were to say to another that he—the speaker —was at that moment digging in the garden, he would present by suggestion the approximate idea of his digging in the garden at some other time than that referred to, while he might be apprehended as digging rapidly or slowly, and with a spade of one shape or another, according to the particular person it was who was addressed. And when one of the phases combined is risible, as where a person in a house said he was at that moment digging in the garden for apples, the approximate idea suggested would be risible accordingly.

Simple nonsense I should call the result of ingenuity of the first species, exercised in the twofold process of, first, the discovery of conceivable ideas approximating the nonsensical statement, and secondly the verbal representation of them in an inconceivable relation to each other. Except when used as a metaphor, under which circumstances convention gives nonsense a place in the expression of thought, the presentation of a statement of this kind would constitute imperfection in respect of the opinion that it was worth making, an imperfection which would be more or less atoned for if the approximate ideas are in any way of an uncommon description, though I do not know of any such.

Incorrect grammar is a combination of words which presents no distinct idea, conceivable or inconceivable, corresponding to the words in their integrity, but which usually approximates grammatical expression nearly enough to satisfy anyone as to the meaning of the speaker or writer; those who themselves are accustomed to use incorrect grammar in the same direction being ignorant even of the verbal dubiety existing. All incorrect grammar would constitute exhibition of inferior acquirements, while such as was not comprehended would, as involving expenditure of the speaker's time without return, also indicate imperfection of Sect. I., Class I.; producing like imperfection in the auditor.

What are called bulls, together with other propositions admitting of reductions to the impossible by more or less complex processes of thought, are, as inconceivable propositions, forms of nonsense. From the contradiction of ideas being more or less recondite, such ideas do not necessarily appear to everyone, as they are, exclusive of each other; and on this account the presentation of complex nonsense would constitute exhibition of mental inferiority—intrinsic or adventitious only according to whether the contradiction of ideas is or is not recondite enough to escape the average individual—with of course more or less evidence of probability or otherwise of the statement being made with knowledge of the contradiction of ideas, according to circumstances.

In virtue of the excuse for the error, these imperfections possess circumstantial novelty No. 1. (class I.).

We have a bull, in which, however, the contradiction of ideas is so near the surface that it would not be likely to be made seriously by any one, in the advice of a man to a friend to escape certain money difficulties by paying his debts with his principal and living on the interest([17]). Since the word interest means a return by another for the possession of money which was previously ours, the possession of the money by us excludes the reception of interest upon that money. But this exclusion of the one idea by the other is not on the surface. While for either one's principal or one's interest to have a twofold existence—for one to enjoy either twice over—would be plainly seen to be contradictory propositions, the fact that principal and interest, from the meaning of the latter word, cannot be enjoyed by the same person at once is not plainly apparent: the ability to select either form of enjoyment of his money might be confounded by the superficial thinker with the ability to choose both. It is this ability or option which forms the excuse for the error. Another bull is seen in a story of a man who had been hauling up a rope for some time without finding the end of it, and exclaimed, "There seems no end to this rope. I believe someone must have cut it off" ([18]).

A rope may be endless in one sense, viz., as regards a piece of it which was its end at a previous time, and it is this circumstance of general affinity with the statement that the rope is endless in a complete sense which forms the excuse for the latter statement.

Like items of simple nonsense, absurdities, *i.e.*, propositions conceivable but incredible of realization because opposed to all experience and principles of reason, are due to ingenuity of the first species (when not presented in connection with the "events of an occasion") and carry positive evidence of the ingenuity; the statement containing a nominal falsehood if the proposition is asserted to be a fact, or belief is expressed in its being reasonably possible of realization. The falsehood involves a risible phase in the utterer in the shape of useless expenditure of time (imperfection of Sect. I., Class I.) in making a statement which no one would credit. The search for and presentation of an absurdity would constitute a mental imperfection (Sect. I., Class II.) by reason of the idea being presumably worthless, as not reasonably possible of realization. The idea, however, may have extraordinariness of character or a greater or less superficial appearance of being reasonably possible of realization—or the two combined—and in proportion to the degree in which it may show these features would the imperfection just mentioned be atoned for.

An idea with both these features is seen in the story of Baron Munchausen's tethering his horse, one snowy night, to what he took for a post, and finding in the morning when the snow had melted that the supposed post was no other than the church steeple, to which the horse was hanging ([19]).

Section II.—Various divergences from conditions familiar to the observer, and various alterations in the existing state of things, that is, various innovations. Many divergences from familiar conditions do not represent actual imperfection, but have the appearance of doing so because of limited experience on the part of the observer. As regards alterations in the existing state of things, we likewise instinctively come to regard the present state of affairs as the most suitable, whence alterations have an appearance of risible imperfection. The first steam engine or bicycle must have had some appearance of the ludicrous (attributed, of course to the constructor) to the observer, though, perhaps, curiosity would have been the first feeling experienced. New fashions in dress, and such an innovation as the first umbrella, would have a more pronounced appearance of imperfection from the circumstance of their association with the human body, and the consequently more especially physical aspect of the inferiority. To the untravelled individual, foreign costumes would present imperfection of this section.

Section III.—Inferiority in special walks of life to the generality of those engaged in such directions.

The following lines on Didactics in poetry give an illustration:—

> Parnassus' peaks still catch the sun,
> But why, O lyric brother,
> Why build a pulpit on the one,
> A platform on the other! [21]

Didactics, proper enough elsewhere, are here regarded as, when introduced into poetry, placing the author as a poet in a position of inferiority to his fellow poets.

Two lines by Pope in reference to a Lord Mayor's Show give another instance, in the shape of almost immediate oblivion of a poet's works:—

> " Now night descending, the proud scene is o'er,
> But lives in Settle's numbers one day more." [22]

## RISIBLE PHASES (CLASS II.). 233

This imperfection is also a phase of circumstantial novelty No. 2, group 7, division 2; the idea which would occur to the mind ordinarily when the subject of the commemoration of an event by a recognized poet was before it being a life of the poem for some substantial period.

Artemus Ward, referring in one of his lectures to some animals in a picture which had been brought out for comment as part of the entertainment, said to the audience, "You may wonder what these are. They are horses. I know it, for the artist told me so himself. He came to me one day and said, 'Mr. Ward, I can conceal it from you no longer. They are horses'" [23].

The inferiority belonging to this Section—the artistic defect in the total failure to represent the horses—is of course not a feature of any interest. The value of the passage lies in the artist's want of common sense in thinking (as is indicated by the words "I can conceal it no longer," which imply that there is temptation for him to keep the secret) that while he retained his secret he would, as would the holder of a secret ordinarily, be in a position of unqualified superiority in respect of that item of knowledge to those who were without it, whereas the circumstance that no one knows the intended species of the animals but himself is most discreditable to him as a painter. It is true the artist's work remains the same, whether or not the secret is kept, but the statement of what the animals are intended for is an item of a certain value, for the interest of every picture is to some extent in its representative aspect—the mental ideas called up by the work—and not only in its presentative aspect—an arrangement of form and colour.

This latter imperfection in the artist is a phase possessing circumstantial novelty No. 1 (class I.), the excuse for the imperfection being the circumstance that secrets ordinarily place the holders in a position of unqualified superiority to those without the knowledge.

Section IV.—Inferiority attributed in idea, in virtue of an ideal incident, to the Deity; and inferiority, also ideal, ascribed to Nature, regarded as a personality.

Inferiority attributed in idea to the Deity is shown in those ideal events which imply in him capability short of the omnipotence which we attributed to him. The believer is accustomed to associate the idea of omnipotence with the idea of a Deity, while the agnostic, although his mind rejects the belief in the real existence of a Deity, entertains the idea of a God, with omnipotence as his attribute, from seeing it done by the believer; and thus all persons refer every idea of a proceeding indicating less than omnipotence in the Deity of the believer, to that fullest measure of power.

An instance ([24]) of this inferiority is seen in the incident No. 1, Chapter VI., Part III. The supposition of the loss of an archangel from heaven is an imputation of power short of omnipotence in the Deity. In Gibbon's *Decline and Fall of the Roman Empire*, Chapter 59, we have another instance of this ideal inferiority. The enemy of the Church (Frederic II.) "is accused . . . of indulging a profane thought that if Jehovah had seen the kingdom of Naples He never would have selected Palestine for the inheritance of His chosen people" ([25]). Here there is a very considerable item of imperfection, presented in the idea that Jehovah, by His ignorance of Naples, is not only less than omniscient, but is without an item of knowledge which is a widely existent possession among mere mortals.

We have an instance ([26]) of inferiority ascribed to Nature, in the witticism by Douglas Jerrold quoted elsewhere: "Nature must have had a very bad pen"—in writing honest man upon some one's face. The inferiority, I should say, is loss of dignity in Nature's engaging in the manual process of writing with a pen. The imperfection, it is true, would be ascribed to Nature whenever we use the metaphorical expression of her writing, but since convention ignores the details of metaphor when that is used in the ordinary way, and regards only the essential feature—here the indication of character—the imperfection would be then ignored.

Section V.—Humour in inanimate objects. This would be shown (1) in certain real or ideal proceedings in or in conformity with the actual course of events, viz., motions or positions which are not in accordance with the conformation of the objects, and (2) in certain ideal self-instituted proceedings taken by these objects endowed by us in imagination with life and powers of outward activity. As regards the firstly mentioned incidents, it seems to me we ascribe a personality to the objects, and observe humour in them upon the same principles as those upon which undignified bodily procedure in man is humorous. Imperfection of the second category, I should say, forms two divisions. The first is that of spontaneous action in general, *i.e.*, powers of thought and bodily movement, and vocal power, which it seems to me we should regard as causing a loss of dignity by these objects on account of spontaneous action being not in accordance with their nature. The proceedings composing the second division are those identical in character with those which would be risible in human beings, and which, as we should regard the objects as having

## RISIBLE PHASES (CLASS II.). 237

the same purposes and capacities for pleasure and pain as ourselves, would appear risible in them. Thus the pot accusing the kettle of blackness ([27]) shows mental inferiority in thinking itself æsthetically superior to the kettle. The footstool, if it declared itself the most important piece of furniture in the house ([28]), would likewise show mental inferiority. Physically, again, they might be imagined as suffering loss and pain like human beings.

It will be observed from the foregoing, taken in connection with Sect. VII., Class I., that where the appropriation of an article to another use than its ordinary one (imperfection of the section just named) involves the movement of it in a manner not suited to its conformation, we have two forms of imperfection, one on the part of man, from his being interested in the appropriation of things to their proper uses, and one on the part of the object itself, in respect of the movement unsuited to its conformation.

# CHAPTER X.

### DETAILED ILLUSTRATION OF RISIBLE PHASES.
### (CLASS III.)

My third class of imperfection — incongruous juxtaposition—has two divisions: one formed of incidents where there are presented in association two of certain attributes, qualities, or characteristics, of animate or inanimate beings, or proceedings of animate beings, which are incongruous with each other from being considerable divergences in opposite directions from the mean or central division of a common scale to which the associated phases belong, this division of incongruous incidents being that of incongruity with diametrical opposition : the other is that of phases incongruous without presenting diametrical opposition, and formed of bathos and anachronisms.

Whether or not all phases in opposite divisions of a common scale can be said to present some incongruity, I do not venture to say; but generally speaking, the only diametrically opposed phases which in juxtaposition present any appreciable incongruity are either those which are of a physical nature, or phases one or each of which is itself a risible imperfection. I have gained but a very imperfect knowledge of this subject—diametrical opposition—but, I hope, enough for the purpose of my analysis.

Under the term bathos I include all sudden changes from poetical, elevated, and intense, sentiment, to an ordinary plane of emotion. The descent, or transition, may be made in two ways; by means of a risible phase (not, however, a mere loss without any characteristic feature; such a phase, of course, would not change the plane of emotion) or by means of certain serious phases of life, limited to the ordinary plane of emotion, of which I will attempt to specify one class—those which produce incongruity in poetry, and which are perhaps all that call for any remark. They are, it seems to me, the greater proportion, perhaps the whole number, of conventional phases of modern origin (though often it may be only particular phases which are incongruous with particular sentiments) their conventionality limiting them to the ordinary plane of emotion, and they thus having a particular place in life, unlike the wholly natural, the unconventional, phases, which appropriately find place in any emotional level.

Such terms as hunger, war, famine, time, represent wholly natural ideas, while the correlative expressions dinner, military offices, famine fund, and so many minutes past a certain hour, are conventional. To some extent conventional expressions may properly find entrance in poetry, the admissible terms being mainly either those which are more general in their character, as the hours, battalions, artillery, or those whose primary use is mainly confined to the past, as a corslet or a pasty (a word introduced without incongruity in Lord Tennyson's *Audley Court*) which fact it would seem has the effect of precluding the appearance of the ordinary which would attach to modern names for these objects.

Anachronisms are opposed phases because these were never found in association in real life. The incongruity here may be described as not an intrinsic but an extrinsic opposition, due to the course of events, which brings various things into existence at different times.

I have now to state why incongruities are risible imperfections. In procedure within the scales of attributes, qualities, or characteristics, incongruous in opposition ; in matters of poetical, grave, or deep sentiment; and in respect of the period at which one may represent an incident or object

## RISIBLE PHASES (CLASS III.). 241

as actually occurring or existing (this being of course no other than a question of truth—or at least substantial accuracy—or misrepresentation); progress, and preservation of welfare is normally attained by the association of like things with like, as regards poetry, etc., and anachronisms, and in the other procedure, by the association of phases not opposed to each other. The generality more or less correctly apprehends the violations of this law—the incongruous phases of procedure—, and thus refers the incongruity to the higher standard of the congruous procedure which it apprehends.

The inability to perceive an incongruity would constitute an ordinary mental inferiority (Sect. I., Class II.).

I have now a few incidental remarks to make respecting incongruous juxtaposition, after which various illustrations of these imperfections will be given; and I must here state that I have not succeeded in all cases in apprehending the direction in which the loss from an incongruity lies.

The person or persons experiencing partial or total loss of progress, or diminution of welfare, in consequence of an incongruity, would, when the phases opposed belong to two sentient beings, be these latter, and sometimes also the observer according to the particular character of the phases opposed, though perhaps in all cases the observer may be said to experience loss to some extent, though it may be inappreciable. Where the phases opposed belong to inanimate objects, the loss would, as might be presumed, be that of the observer. With opposed physical attributes, as where tall persons associate with short, stout with lean, robust with weak, the loss would mainly be on the part of those persons. Tall and short men would experience the various physical inconveniences of being on greatly different levels of altitude, stout and lean persons various inconveniences which I presume must attend movements by them of greatly different degrees of rapidity, and the association of robust and weak persons would, I should say, cause a loss from their difference in power rendering them unable to co-operate to the best advantage for each. While the observer may be said to incur some slight loss in the extra energy required to adjust the focus of the material eye to persons differing greatly in girth or stature, and his mental focus in the observation of opposed attributes less visible, or invisible, to the outward eye. Where the incongruity is in a production, transient or permanent, by a single individual, or a joint production by more than one person, as bathos in poetry, or incongruity with diametrical opposition in any work of art, the loss, I should say, would be the author's only. Presumably paying no more than the positive value of the production, the recipient of the production does not lose welfare in the direction of over payment for it. But the author—who may or may not perceive the incongruity in his production—loses; by reason of a production presenting incongruity being of less exchangeable value than one, otherwise equally good, without incongruity.

Where the observer is a loser by an incongruity there is, it would seem, little if any prominence in his imperfection, from the circumstance that it is not one indicating inferior capabilities in him, and perhaps also because his loss is never great. And it appears to me that, while recognizing the force of the incongruity, the observer yet in idea dissociates himself substantially from risible imperfection; *i.e.*, entertains no thought of any risible imperfection in himself.

With artificial objects presenting incongruity when brought into association, sometimes the opposition is in their intrinsic attributes, as in the juxtaposition of a delicate piece of glass work with a heap of hard, coarse articles, a ball dress with a sack, and sometimes in ideas of which the objects are symbolical or representative, as a crown and punch bowl, a spelling book and a volume of Plato or Aristotle.

The following are a few illustrations of incongruous juxtaposition.

The first is the association of gravity, or exceptional seriousness, and jocularity of subject matter; an extract from a report of an imaginary concert. "The concert was concluded by a piece called 'Life in Death and Death in Life,' a symbolical work, showing how all things intermingle; how we pass from childhood to maturity and again into childhood; how the beginning and the end are one. In witness whereof it was pointed out after the performance that the music which had just drawn tears from every eye would have been equally effective if turned upside down and begun at the end; while the libretto, which moved the very soul with its solemn pathos, could be planted, as it were, tail upwards, without the least injury to its vitality "[1].

The phrase "In witness whereof"—being a stereotyped form of expression in legal documents, has the appearance of having a prescriptive right to be confined to these, and thus its employment elsewhere has the appearance of inferiority from being a violation of conventional propriety (imperfection of Sect. I., Class II.).

The following two lines from a Christmas card are at opposite ends of the scale of fluency of verbal rhythm :—

> "Ye compliments of ye seasonne I bring,
> And wish you joy in everything"[2].

Over and above the contrast between the remarkable fluency of the second line and the even more remarkable defects in the progression of the first, it seems to me that the second carries with it a suggestion—a ring as of triumphal achievement in the poet's having done this much, viz., constructed his line—the first—albeit two inadmissible syllables remain as traces of the struggle, or at least one. In such case there would be presented a further incongruity in the juxtaposition of the author's feeling of triumph with the emotion which would occur to the reader as that appropriate to the occasion, viz., a sense of inferiority.

Incongruity would seem to lie in an attempt at injustice resulting in the reversal of the hoped for relations between the parties concerned, by the person making the attempt being deprived even of property legitimately his own—a proceeding described by the metaphorical phrase, "the biter bit," where, as I suppose it often does, this means "the would be biter bit." The mean division of the scale to which the opposed phases belong would be the absence or the frustration of attempt at injustice.

A common form of incongruity is the opposition between want of dignity, or, as is often the case, procedure by persons, such as children, and those of low station, whose position is such as to require little or no sacrifices to be made for its maintenance, and what we call an oppressive sense of dignity (a phase involved in, though I suppose it does not wholly constitute,—is only a part of, pompousness) which would seem to be, strictly speaking, superfluous concession for the maintenance of one's station. These contrasts present diametrical opposition in the scale of concessions made to dignity; the mean of the scale being a due amount of dignity, and the opposing divisions being want of it and superfluous concessions to it. In the scale of dignity itself the normal degree of perfection is the maximum degree; dignity relating to broad and general principles, which place perfection within the power of everyone, and hence there can be there no divergence from the normal condition except in one direction—that of diminution.

The following is an instance of deep emotion in the form of great lamentation without adequate cause (preventing any appeal to sympathy, even if the loss were not, as it is, deserved) found in association with considerable humour. One of Mr. George Grossmith's impersonations is that of a connoisseur in old china, whose occupations extend to the fabrication of spurious antiquities in this material. This individual, after a long and intent inspection of an article he has given a high price for in the belief that it was a genuine antiquity, bursts out, in a tone of intensest anguish, "It's my own make!" [3] The humour in association with the emotional phase is the error of judgment made by the connoisseur in taking his own handiwork for a genuine antiquity; and there is a further item of humour of especial prominence (imperfection of Sect. I., Class II.) in his apparent inability to perceive the incongruity.

In the admixture of comedy with tragedy, on the stage, which may occasionally be made with good effect, the opposing characteristics are not both at the ends of their respective divisions of the common scale, the comedy being slight and delicate, and thus having only a minimum breadth of jocularity.

Most parodies present incongruous juxtaposition, those which do so consisting in the expression, in a more or less close approximation to the words of some poetical train of thought, of ideas incongruous with it either from being confined to the exclusively ordinary plane of emotion, or from going beyond this—presenting inferiority in themselves. Their justification usually lies in the existence of some slight imperfection or, it may be, innovation upon precedent in the original, which feature the parody makes broadly defective by exaggeration, or by presentation under different conditions than those of the original. The work parodied, not being actually presented, is only suggested by the parody, and it thus needs acquaintance with the original to recognise a second and incongruous train of thought, unless, that is, elevated passages are interspersed in the parody itself.

## CHAPTER XI.

### SATIRE, IRONY, AND SARCASM.

SATIRE, irony, and sarcasm, of which latter I should say ridicule by jeers and mimicry is a form, of a less dignified character, I should call the divisions of a category the distinguishing feature of which is the observation of a twofold element in procedure by a person or persons; viz., moral inferiority, not passing certain limits, and risible inferiority, not limited in degree, and always of some amount of prominence.

I should describe satire as the exposure of combined moral and, in one or more directions, risible imperfections in procedure, by a person or persons, distinguished by the following feature, viz., that its real character is more or less recondite, and is on this account liable to pass unperceived by the generality of persons without special study by them, or, where the real nature of the case is exceptionally recondite, without an exposition of the circumstances by someone of exceptional insight, as the professed satirist is or assumes to be.

The moral inferiority lies in such directions as unwarranted pretensions to a position of moral or intellectual superiority over others; pretensions to a position of moral or intellectual equality with others, unwarranted by reason of the presence of moral or intellectual inferiority in the claimant; and expenditure on self, or self indulgence, to an extent which the satirist thinks should be regarded as culpable. The risible inferiority necessarily shown is the false estimate of one's moral or intellectual status (adventitious inferiority, of Sect. I. Class I. of risible phases) resulting from the ignorance either that one is no better than others, morally or otherwise; that one fails to reach a position of moral or other equality with others by reason of the existence of moral or other inferiority; or that the expenditure or self indulgence noted by the satirist is culpable.

Of risible inferiorities in other directions — imperfections not necessarily existent in the material for satire—I may mention the meanness —a want of dignity — of snobbism, of which Thackeray discovered or professed to discover so much.

Perhaps one illustration of satire will be enough —Thackeray's dictum that the conduct of George the Fourth was destructive of the claim made for

## SATIRE, IRONY, AND SARCASM. 251

him, and acquiesced in by him, of his being the first gentleman in Europe, and even deprived him of any claim to the name of gentleman ([1]). There is noted here moral inferiority in the unwarranted pretension to superiority in the qualities constituting a gentleman, and risible inferiority in the shape of ignorance that the pretension is unwarranted.

Irony, in what seems to me may be regarded as the strict sense of the word, is the attempt at indication to another, by inference from a process of exaggeration, not expressly by words, of one's sense of the exhibition by the other of imperfection in the shape of mental inferiority, or mental and moral inferiority combined. The exaggeration is to such an extent as to be obvious to persons in general, thus forming a phase of circumstantial novelty No. 2 (see Obvious Exaggerations, Chapt. VI., Part III.), and is, according to circumstances, either an exaggerated representation of the procedure itself, or the presentation in idea, as probable of realization, of procedure similar to it but exaggerated in degree; the exaggeration in this latter category not necessarily taking the same precise direction as the procedure noted, but on occasion merely the same general direction.

Where it is reasonably possible that a

particular individual, as distinguished from persons in general, should regard the representation as a true one, or the ideal procedure as probable of realization, there is formal presumptive evidence of ingenuity of the third species, while where the exaggeration is to such an extent that it is not reasonably possible that he should so regard it, the evidence of ingenuity is positive.

The solely risible imperfections noted by irony do not, as will perhaps have been observed, belong to this category, relating as it does to acts in which moral inferiority is shown; but since they are so rarely met with, I have, to avoid making a specific distinction in the heading of this chapter, as also the repetition of general remarks on irony, made my reference to these incidents here. We have an instance of this form of irony if a person, eating with a gravy spoon (exhibition of inferiority of acquirement in respect of conventional custom), were recommended to use a soup ladle instead ([2]).

The combined risible and moral imperfections forming the usual material for irony are such as an act or a demand by a person, or an accredition to himself, which is considered by another unjust; or a request put forward by the former as reasonable, and considered by the other to be unreasonable, and, in consequence, to involve injustice from its implying a charge of injustice in the person of whom the request is made, if he holds, as he then would, that justice does not demand a compliance with the request.

The risible imperfection noted by irony I should term an error, or imputed error of opinion, indicating intrinsic mental inferiority.

The ridicule by irony of these combined mental and moral imperfections may be regarded as constituting two divisions, the irony of resentment, and good-humoured irony, the latter being shown when the speaker thinks there are circumstances such as youth, or want of education or experience, which excuse the imperfection.

The following are among the more ordinary forms of irony. It may take the shape of an exaggeration of the particular character of the unjust proposition, as when, in answer to what one thought some immoderate request for alms, he were to say "Perhaps you would like my whole fortune?" [3]. Another form is the extension of the characteristic of absence of inferiority assumed for procedure by the author, and, as the observer thinks, unwarrantably, to the characteristic of excellence. Irony of this kind would be shown if a person speaking of some performance of his, considered by another to be of an inferior description, and for which the most that he himself would claim would be that it reached the average level of merit, were to assert that it did not fall below that level, and were to receive the reply, "I think you have made an exceptional exhibition of ability." (⁴). A third form of irony is a mere expression of agreement with another, accompanied by the tone of voice indicative of irony. Although in this form of irony there is professedly no exaggeration, I should say that an admission of the objectionable proposition in any other way than by silence implies some exaggeration of it. An expressed agreement with the other's position seems to me to carry some such implication as that, without doubt, or with but little doubt, he is right; a stronger position I think it may be assumed, than that held by him.

Using the word irony, as I have done, in the limited sense of the attempt by inference from exaggeration to bring a person to a recognition of an unsuspected deficiency in him, any ridicule addressed to a person for deficiency of which he is aware would be classed as a variety of sarcasm, viz., taunts, even those jocular inversions substituting excellences for defects, which we commonly call irony. It would perhaps be more correct to describe what I have regarded as irony in general, by the specific term of "the irony of attempted enlightenment," thus leaving the other

## SATIRE, IRONY, AND SARCASM. 255

specific term, "the irony of taunt," for a proportion of taunts, viz., those which are not faithful representations of defects—plain jeers—, but phases of circumstantial novelty No. 2, in the shape of inversions and improbable or else absurd explanations (Group No. 7, Division 1, 1st Variety; and Group 11). This, of course, would leave the three divisions presented in this chapter unaffected except by an alteration in name (viz., the alteration to satire, the irony of enlightenment, and sarcasm, a variety of which, viz., taunts, is composed of the ingenious and the non-ingenious descriptions). But as it would necessitate a further and heterogeneous class, formed of division 2 and a part of division 3, I have used the word irony in the foregoing exclusive sense of attempt at enlightenment.

The distinguishing characteristics of sarcasm, separating it from satire and irony, are, I should say, the obvious nature to persons in general of the imperfection noted—differentiating sarcasm from satire, where the character of the procedure noted is more or less recondite —; and the circumstance—this differentiating it from irony—that it is not the attempt at indication of a defect by the inference which an obvious exaggeration should bear.

Conceit, vanity, and such affectations as are

obvious to the generality of persons, form probably the bulk of the material for sarcasm. Of the several forms which sarcasm takes, the lower are such taunts and jeers as are not phases of circumstantial novelty No. 2; while the higher descriptions are mainly found where circumstantial novelty is presented in the ridicule.

That description of witty retort which destroys a position of superiority to or equality with others, unwarrantably assumed by a person, pertains, by reason of the moral inferiority in such undue assumption, to the present category and division, as well as to the group it may belong to in virtue of presenting a phase of circumstantial novelty No. 2.

The material for sarcasm in such incidents is, we find, in the moral inferiority which unwarranted assumption of superiority to or equality with others constitutes, and in the intellectual inferiority—error of judgment—involved in the ignorance that the assumption is unwarranted.

There is, however, a further feature in these cases which would be instinctively felt to be absent from sarcasm in its other forms; this feature being a risible imperfection of decided prominence. It consists in the error of judgment made by the presuming individual in thinking his right to his assumption would probably remain, not perhaps accepted, but not denied under conditions giving material weight to the denial, as is the case when the denial is accompanied by evidence of a superiority in its author, as is the appreciable wit of these retorts. While another feature, correlative with this, would be our pleasure at finding the claim thus effectually denied—a pleasure, of course, of a different kind to that which we take in the wit of the remark, one being a moral and the other an intellectual emotion.

The following incident would come within the province of sarcasm like the foregoing, if we hold, as we probably should, that the words of the subject of the witticism imply an unwarranted assumption of superiority over the average individual. To those, however, who thought otherwise—that no such unwarranted assumption was implied by the words—the only features would be an item of risible imperfection, of no great prominence, which will be specified, and the wit in the retort.

The joke, it will be observed, is one which is suggested by a very obvious inference, but not actually presented, *i.e.*, made, since the words which convey the joke have no actual connection, though a very obviously intended one, with the first speaker's words. In the old Irish Parliament a member in the course of a speech gave utterance to the words "I am the guardian of my own honour," whereon another member started up with the interruption "I had always understood that the gentleman who has just been speaking was an enemy to sinecures" ([5]). The first speaker's words are—though only by force of license—a general expression, bearing the two interpretations of the guardianship of an actually existent property, and the care of one that is fictitious—a sinecure. It bears the latter interpretation by license only because the word sinecure is not a term ever generally recognized as applying to a (fictitious) mental quality. The quibble here is not in the shape of an expressed, but an understood assertion that the other's guardianship of his honour is a sinecure—that what he calls his honour has no substance, but is a meaningless phrase. We perceive the understood assertion because the words come as an interruption to the other's speech immediately after his reference to his honour, and mean, if they mean anything in connection with that reference, that the speaker's attitude of enmity to sinecures was inconsistent with the guardianship he held.

If, as I interpret the first speaker's words, they constitute a claim to decide, without reference to any opinions of others, what is honourable conduct for him and what is not, there is of course presumption shown in the shape of an unwarranted assumption of superiority over at least the average

## SATIRE, IRONY, AND SARCASM. 259

individual, who makes no such claim for himself, and also over such persons admittedly superior to the average individual as do not make the claim for themselves. If this is not the proper interpretation of the words, the claim made, in which I assume there is no presumption, would be that the speaker shall be trusted to do nothing dishonourable. Whether a presumptuous claim is held to be made or not, there is error of the same kind as in the previous incident, viz., in the opinion that such claim as is made would be likely to meet with no denial carrying material weight in virtue of its being accompanied by wit. But if we thought a just claim had been made, the special pleasure in another's discomfiture which we should feel on an occasion like that of the previous incident would be absent here.

Besides the above error of judgment there is another risible imperfection, of no great prominence, by reason of the jester ostensibly having withdrawn at some period—the intimation of the circumstance being only made now, and the inferiority from the loss of esteem being thus only exhibited now—the credit for ordinary honour which reason points out is the due of everyone not proved dishonourable.

There is another version of this joke which represents the interruption as taking the form "I must then congratulate the gentleman who has just been speaking on the sinecure which he possesses." This form of the joke—a positive ascription, not mere inference, of possession of a sinecure—presents a difference from the other in that the jest is made in words, instead of being suggested only, by obvious inference.

I should describe a taunt as the calling attention to a failure in another to make good a claim which appeared problematical, and therefore unjust, from the probabilities at the time of the claim not being in its favour. The language of Elijah to the prophets of Baal unavailingly invoking their god, in which he urges them to cry louder, for perhaps the god slept or was taking a walk ([6]), although sometimes called irony, and under any circumstances having certain features in common with it, would under my definitions be classed as a taunt; since when Elijah spoke, the great probability of the presumptuous nature, from having no foundation, of the claim that they were favoured by a god Baal, was seen by the prophets themselves—did not remain to be indicated by the inference carried by irony.

When Elijah speaks it is not yet shown that the prophets of Baal are favoured to no extent by a potent god, for, though tardily, he may yet answer their appeal. But as he does not readily answer, every probability points to no response ever coming, and thus, though a tardy answer is yet

## SATIRE, IRONY, AND SARCASM. 261

possible, not even a claim to that much would, in the face of so great probability against its being substantiated, be now made ; that is, there is no remnant of unsuspected presumption for Elijah to discover to the prophets when he speaks his memorable words.

The explanation of the cause of the absence of a response pertains to the group of phases of circumstantial novelty No. 2 which have an invariable immediate unlimited class connection with the events of the occasion, but which belong to class 1 of the phases of novelty because, while not being reasonably possible of representing reality, they have legitimacy of presentation by license, viz., by the extravagance of imagination permitted by the laws of ridicule.

# CHAPTER XII.

### MISCELLANEOUS.

In this last chapter is made, *inter alia,* such brief reference as seems called for to that form of wit, or so-called wit, which is not ingenuity, but consists in acuteness of observation in association with terseness of expression; and mention of various sources of extrinsic value in risible phases, other than value proceeding from circumstantial novelty, incongruous juxtaposition, or rhythm and rhyme.

The form of wit referred to, it need scarcely be said, is that shown in all proverbs, aphorisms, and maxims, and nothing more need be said of these than that they sometimes present risible phases, in a variety of forms, and are sometimes without these. Such proverbs as contain metaphors, as, for instance, A rolling stone gathers no moss ([1]), add to the wit of this description, ingenuity of the first species, in virtue of the invention of the metaphor.

## MISCELLANEOUS.

As to the above-mentioned extrinsic sources of value in risible phases;—the accumulation of risible phases all bearing upon one subject generally gives to the incident as a whole a worth considerably beyond the mere aggregate of the value of each risible phase taken independently.

Another source of value in risible phases would seem to be discrimination or restraint in the matter of intentional exaggeration, whereby as close an appearance of reality is given as is compatible with marked exaggeration. One of Lamb's letters to Landor, given in Forster's life of the latter, presents an instance. "I knew your Welsh annoyancers, the measureless Beethams," he writes; "I knew a quarter of a mile of them. Seventeen brothers and sixteen sisters, as they appear to me in memory" (²). The risible phases here are: first, exhibition of defective common sense in regarding a family according to their aggregate measurements: and secondly, the enormous number of the family, as stated (imperfection of Sect. II., Class II.). In the words "a quarter of a mile," we have one of the lower, if not of the lowest, of one description of measurements—that used for determining travelling distances—which moderation gives as near an appearance of reality as is possible to the large exaggeration employed. (The assertion that the family measured a quarter of a mile is, as an exaggeration obvious to anyone, a phase of circumstantial novelty No. 2, the event of the occasion being simply the mention of the family.) And again, by his addition to the, in all probability, exaggerated statement as to the number of the family, of the words " as they appear to me in memory," the writer invests a remarkably exaggerated statement with that aspect of the natural—of being made with serious intent—which from the fallibility of the memory a statement respecting the distant past may have when it would seem but an intentional exaggeration if the knowledge of the facts were of recent acquisition.

Magnitude of interests affected is another source of special value in a risible phase. Illustration No. 22, Chapter VI., Part II., where a whole field of competitors in a race have been kept at the utmost stretch of attention, and then find themselves without any definite prospect of beginning the race (imperfection of Sect. III., Class I.), gives an instance ([3]) of this.

Lastly is to be mentioned a class of errors, of which I have already given one or two specimens, chiefly in Chapter IX., but which call for some reference here on account of their large number. This is the class of mistakes which have a special value, as humour, from their being due to questions being regarded from an individual standpoint, this making wholly natural mistakes which would not be so if their authors had only the general point of view from which to contemplate matters. These errors, which scarcely need any illustration here, may, I suppose, be divided into the two categories of those caused by the bias of self-interest in general, and those due to a person's having some special interest or occupation; such as, to quote here an imperfection of the latter kind, the view of literature taken by the publisher who was reported to have said of a deceased author, whose books he brought out, "Yes, I am right sorry he has gone. He was an old man, but there was a good deal of meat left on him" ([4])— a speech which is not confined to the legitimate contemplation of literature solely in the subordinate aspect with which the publishing interest is concerned, but shows no recognition whatever of literature having any other aspect than this— refers to an author as if his one use, the one purpose of his existence, was that of yielding meat for his publisher.

It will be seen how under such a theory of risible imperfection as mine, the broader differences which mark the humour of writers noted for this quality are in every way accounted for, though of course it does not need an original theory to explain some of them. The humour of the satirist shows the two distinctive features that it consists in imperfection in others, not himself, and is exhibited in conjunction with the moral inferiority I have specified in Chapter XI.

The humour presented intentionally by the dramatic writer (always slight and well short of the ludicrous, avoiding thereby pronounced incongruity) by the writers of comedy and farce, and by novelists who deal in the quality, shows the former of the above-mentioned features, viz., the imperfection being on the part of others, not the obvious inventor of it. While those writers who show humour in the relation of their own reflections, opinions, and experiences, often to a large extent exhibit the imperfection in themselves, chiefly by way of general mental inferiority, and not seldom in the form of incongruous juxtaposition. With the question as to the precise province of the specific term humour, my theory, it will have been seen, is not concerned, recognizing the matter as one of individual preference — a preference which, it need scarcely be said, with most persons lies in one or other of two directions only, viz., on the one hand the refusal of the name of humour to any risible incident, however ingenious, if it is wanting in one or more of certain requirements such as truth to nature, pathos, and the less definable qualities of felicity, propriety of application, and tone; and on the other hand, the acceptance of a substantial measure of ingenuity as in itself a qualification for the title of humour.

Here, then, ends my theory. An indefinite amount of further illustration might have been given, and undoubtedly with advantage in one or two groups (No. 9 for instance) in Chapter VI., in which chapter, moreover, it may be held that as regards two of the lesser groups (Nos. 6 and 10) I have not established the application to them of my theory of circumstantial novelty (2nd description) in a wholly satisfactory manner. I am fain to believe, however, that the fundamental and general features of the whole theory are satisfactory, and that, except in the chapter just mentioned, I can scarcely be charged with any very substantial shortcomings. While with regard to Chapter VI., I cannot but think that the treatment of even a proportion only of the groups with completeness, and congruity with my theory of ingenuity—which, if I judge my work rightly, may at least be claimed—may be enough for a convincing theory.

THE END.

# INDEX.

Absurdities:

Due to ingenuity of 1st species when not presented in connection with the events of an occasion: 51-2, 230.

When so presented, due to ingenuity of 3rd species: 62, l. 8; 81, l. 8; and 159-61.

The election to seek and present an "absurdity" (whether connected with the event of an occasion or not) constitutes mental inferiority, of degree short of defective common sense: 62, l. 13-26; 230, l. 28, to 231, l. 3.

Adventitious inferiorities: Occasional references: 21; 46, l. 7-13; 60, l. 18, to 61, l. 8.

Errors of judgment:

1st Division: data for correct conclusion accessible: 208-9; 212, l. 14, to 214, l. 15.

2nd Division: such data not accessible: 209, l. 12, to 217, l. 14.

Errors of opinion: 217.

Antitheses (*Phases of Circumstantial Novelty No. 2*):

See Identities and Antitheses.

Apparent attempts at deceit: In general: 28-31; 182, l. 15, to 184, l. 8; 215, l. 19, to 216, l. 24.

Conditions excluding a false statement from the category: 29.

Involve incidental inferiority and adventitious inferiority in the authors: 183, l. 18, to 184, l. 8; 215, l. 19, to 217, l. 5.

Made in connection with "events of occasions" (then forming phases of circumstantial novelty No. 2): See Group No. 7, Division 1, Chap. VI., Pt. II.

# INDEX.

Category of jokes made by a certain inversion of usual processes of jocularity: (*Phases of Circumstantial Novelty No.* 2): Chap. VI., Pt. II.; and (general references) Chap. V.

Contains two classes, viz., inverted quibbles and certain incidents of group No. 7, 1st Division: 143.

Distinguishing characteristics are event of the occasion (provided always by ingenuity of 1st species) being more or less difficult of provision; and phase of novelty (which is not expressed in words) being easily perceptible: 143.

"Generic" imperfections: 150.

Circumstantial Novelty No. 1: *Circumstantial Novelty by reason of excuse for error.* Explained and specifically illustrated; Chaps. V. and VII.

Attaches on occasion to mental inferiorities: 37-8.

Forms two classes: 162.

Excuse for the imperfections in class I. is of two descriptions, according to two senses in which the word is used; viz. (1), excuse in strict sense; (2), a circumstance in the nature of an excuse: 162, l. 18, to 163, l. 21.

Circumstantial Novelty No. 2: *Circumstantial Novelty by reason of remoteness from ordinary mental range.* Explained and specifically illustrated; Chaps. V. and VI.

Attaches on occasion to phases in general, risible and non-risible: 38, l. 3-10.

Phases form two classes, respectively with and without legitimacy of presentation: 39-40.

Class I. divided into phases having special connection with events of occasion: (41, l. 16, to 43, l. 7), and those having a general connection therewith: 43, l. 8-10.

Class II. contains phases of general connection only: 43, l. 11-12.

Where one of these phases presented, incident shows risible phase (termed "generic") in one or more directions: 46, l. 7-13; 59-62.

Phases of special connection are phases definitely presented, wholly or in part, by the events of the occasion: (41,

## INDEX. 271

l. 16-21); and discovery of such phases constitutes subspecies of 3rd species of ingenuity : 8, 36.

These phases definitely presented are, as regards some groups, contained wholly or in part in the events of the occasion; as regards other groups, not contained therein : 41, l. 16, to 42, l. 14.

"Events of the occasion" are provided sometimes in the ordinary course of things ; at other times by ingenuity of 1st species : 48, l. 26, to 49, l. 2.

"Data" or "material," sometimes existing, for events of the occasion : 65-6 ; 101-2 ; 143.

Incidental remarks : 43-8.

Conceit, pride, vanity : 33-4.

"Concomitant and incidental"
event of occasion. (An integral
part of primary event, as regards connection and remoteness of phase of novelty):

Gives (provided it is noticed) an appreciable value to phase of novelty : 43-4.

Instances (Chap. VI., Pt. I.)   *   *   *   *   *   *

Of its being of less immediate presentation than the primary event : Nos. 11 and 12.

Of its being not an actual occurrence, but an intention; or a more or less reasonable presumption : No. 14.

Of its being not necessarily expressed in words when joke made : No. 11.

Of its being not expressed in words before joke made : Nos. 14 and 15.

"Data, or material" (Occasional
antecedent conditions) for
events of occasion :

With the majority of puns an indispensable antecedent; as giving to a twofold rendering merely, a twofold signification : 65, l. 15, to 66.

May precede event, or events, of occasion in group No. 4, but not indispensable here : 101-2.

Are provided (except in Group No. 8) by ingenuity of 1st

species, or in the ordinary course of things, according to circumstances: 66, l. 26-8; 102.

Dishonourable procedure:

Is a non-risible phase in exhibitor as being an injustice to others: (26-34); and risible in him as involving lack of moral dignity: 27, l. 3-7; 198, l. 17-23.

When shown in petty matters involves additional risible phase in exhibitor in shape of lack of intellectual dignity: 28, l. 17-22; 198, l. 24, to 204, l. 2.

Evidence of Ingenuity: Is of various kinds:—Positive; Variable and Indefinite; and Formal presumptive: 52-7.

Positive evidence: 52, l. 17, to 53, l. 6; 55; 56, l. 24, to 57, l. 4.

Variable and indefinite evidence: mainly concerns ingenuity of 2nd species: (53, l. 22, to 54, l. 2), and the provision of "events of the occasion:" 53, l. 10-21. A few phases of circumstantial novelty No. 2 are accompanied by this evidence: 54, l. 7-13; 137.

Formal presumptive evidence confined to various phases of circumstantial novelty No. 2 (52, l. 11-17), and to mental inferiority (ostensible deficiency of common sense) often accompanying presentation of same: 56, l. 18-23.

Where ingenuity is avowed by presenter of phase of circumstantial novelty, avowal constitutes positive evidence, superseding formal presumptive. While, necessarily, above-mentioned mental inferiority is absent: 56, l. 23, to 57, l. 3.

Where phase of circumstantial novelty not reasonably possible of realization, evidence of ingenuity is positive: 55, l. 9-12.

Exaggerations (obvious to persons in general) of excellences, imperfections, or attendant conditions of imperfections. (*Phases of Circumstantial Novelty No. 2*). Chap. VI. Pt. III., and (general references) Chap. V.

## INDEX.

Phases of Exceptional immediate connection with events of the occasion (*Phases of Circumstantial Novelty No.* 2) :   Chap. VI., Pt. II., and (general references) Chap. V.

Falsehoods (Moral inferiorities, real or nominal) :   Chap. IV. *et. seq.*

> Conditions excluding falsehoods from category of attempts at deceit : 29.
>
> Obstruction of legitimate progress, or other risible imperfection, caused in recipient of, or believer in, a falsehood : 29, l. 18, to 30, l. 15 ; 186, l. 28, to 187, l. 9.
>
> Professed but not real disbelief in authenticity of news causes in apparently discredited person exhibition of obstruction of legitimate progress of a particular description : 188, l. 27, to 189, l. 15.
>
> Such imperfection is ostensible merely, if profession of disbelief is obviously unreal : 189, l. 3-10.
>
> Where there was no reasonable chance of credit being given, indicate intellectual, *i.e.*, risible, inferiority as well as moral : 30-1 ; 154, l. 3-12.

"Generic" risible phases in incidents presenting phases of circumstantial novelty No. 2 : 59-62.

> Where discovery of phase of novelty constitutes wit, generic risible phase is error of judgment : 60, l. 18, to 61, l. 8.
>
> Of incidents presenting phases of novelty opposed to common sense (viz., most phases of special connection, and all phases of general connection) the 1st category shows generic risible phase in shape of ostensible mental inferiority (Sect. I., Class II.), or useless expenditure of time (Sect. I., Class I.), according to whether phase of novelty is reasonably possible of realization or not : 62.
>
> 2nd category of such incidents shows one generic risible phase (real mental inferiority of degree short of defective common sense) common to all incidents : 62.

# 274 INDEX.

For generic risible phases in separate groups and any divisions thereof, see the several illustrations of these.

Humour (Intentional):

Instance of "dry" humour given and analysed: 166-70.

Identities and Antitheses: (Chap. VI., Pt. I.; and (*Phases of Circumstantial* (general references) Chap. V. *Novelty No.* 2):

> For phase of novelty to be worth notice, events of the occasion must be of an occasional or transitory character: 97, l. 21, to 98, l. 19.
>
> May be left unindicated when easy of perception: 100, l. 19-23.
>
> Specialities marking certain incidents of the group: 100, l. 23, to 102, l. 11.

Idioms treated from the risible point of view: (*Phases of Circumstantial Novelty No.* 2):

See Metaphors and Idioms.

Incidental inferiorities: 21; 183, l. 27-8; 215, l. 20, to 217, l. 5.

Incongruous juxtaposition: Chap. X.

(Composes Class III. of Imperfection).

Ingenuity in general: Forms three species.

> Description of ideas due to ingenuity of 1st species: 8; 48; 50-2.
>
> Do. as regards ingenuity of 2nd species: 8; 35-6.
>
> Ingenuity of 3rd species consists in discovery (with or without expression—express notice—according to circumstances) of phases of circumstantial novelty No. 2: 8; 36.
>
> Discovery (with or without expression, according to circumstances) of phases definitely presented by events of the occasion, constitutes sub-species of species No. 3: 8; 36.
>
> Suggested reservation of word wit for this sub-species: 36; 49-50.

Evidence of: See Evidence.

Phases of Invariable immediate class connection with events of the occasion: (*Phases of Circumstantial Novelty No.* 2): Chap. VI., Pt. II.; and (general references) Chap V.

# INDEX.

1st Division: 121-37.

    1st Variety: 122-30. A proportion of these, viz., improbable explanations of one's own conduct, do not carry formal presumptive evidence of wit. Variable and indefinite evidence of wit presented or not according to circumstances: 126, l. 7-16.

    Jokes by a certain inversion of usual process illustrated in special category with inverted quibbles: 143-50.

    2nd Variety: 130-7.

    2nd Division ("Humour by surprise"): 137-43.

| | |
|---|---|
| Phases of Invariable immediate unlimited class connection; legitimate of presentation through the license of ridicule: (*Phases of Circumstantial Novelty No.* 2): | Chap. VI., Pt. III. (class I.) and (general references) Chap. V. |
| Ditto; without legitimacy of presentation: | Chap. VI., Pt. III. (class II.); and (general references) Chap. V. |
| Irony: Term used as implying attempt at enlightenment, by inference from obvious exaggeration. (Presents phases of circumstantial novelty No. 2; and also—with unimportant exception, see p. 252—belongs to special category in respect of moral inferiority noted.) | See Satire, Irony, and Sarcasm. |

Laughter: 15, 16.

Metaphors. Due to ingenuity of 1st species: 8; 48.

| | |
|---|---|
| Metaphors and Idioms treated from the risible point of view: (*Phases of Circumstantial Novelty No.* 2): | Chap. VI., Pt. I.; and (general references) Chap. V. |

    Remarks on the legitimate use of metaphors and idioms: 82, l. 24, to 89, l. 16.

    The two grades of jokes on metaphors particularized: 88-9.

276 *INDEX.*

Normal conditions of use of a metaphor and of consideration thereof by recipient : 83, l. 23-7.

When extra-ordinary circumstances accompany use of metaphor, some feature of dissimilarity presents (if noticed) of its own accord (thereby making attention to it more or less appropriate) intrinsic or extrinsic exceptional aspect : 84, l. 2-15 ; 91, l. 23, to 92, l. 16.

When no extra-ordinary circumstances present, production of exceptional aspect (special search being required for this) is only appropriate when a substantial object is attained thereby : 86, l. 5-9 ; 88, l. 27, to 89, l. 5 ; 91, l. 7-23.

Discussion exclusively of risible treatment of metaphors : 89-95.

Specific statement of conditions giving propriety of production to a joke : 91, l. 1, to 92, l. 16.

Extra-ordinary circumstances accompanying use of metaphor constitute " concomitant and incidental " event of the occasion : 92.

Discussion exclusively of risible treatment of Idioms : 95-6.

Nonsense, *i.e.*, an inconceivable proposition ;   A mental inferiority : Chap. IX.

Although an inconceivable proposition, presents by suggestion an approximate conceivable idea : 226-7.

Simple nonsense, due to ingenuity of 1st species : 52.

Complex nonsense (due to ingenuity of 2nd species when wittingly produced) possesses in its commoner form, viz., that of Bulls, circumstantial novelty No.1 : 229.

Phases partly contained in events of occasion : (*Phases of Circumstantial Novelty No.* 2) :   Chap. VI., Pt. I. ; and (general references) Chap. V.

Perfection :

Sense in which this word, and consequently the word imperfection, is used : 12 to 14, l. 6.

Puns : (*Phases of Circumstantial Novelty No.* 2) :   Chap. VI., Pt. I. ; and (general references) Chap. V.

Form two classes ; (1) search for second signification not imperative, (2) search obligatory : 67.

# INDEX.

Whole substantial value consists in provision of event of occasion, with, at times, "data" for same; phase of novelty needing no appreciable wit for its discovery: 64, 66, l. 26-8.

Generic imperfection peculiar to group: 72.

Riddles: (*Mostly Phases of Circumstantial Novelty No. 2*): See Puns (2nd class).

Risible phases: Three general descriptions of these: 11, 12.

    Classified: Chapter III.

    Specifically illustrated: Chaps. VIII., IX., and X.

    Possess intrinsic novelty, and also on occasion extrinsic or circumstantial novelty (Nos. 1 or 2): 16, 17.

    Receive an adventitious value when presented in metre or rhythmical form: 17.

    Serious moral issues often modify or determine effect of observation of these phases: 14; 17; 23-4; 180; 181; 186.

    "Generic" risible phases accompanying phases of circumstantial novelty No. 2: See "Generic."

Sarcasm: (Occasionally presents phases of Circumstantial Novelty No. 2, and also belongs to special category in respect of moral inferiority noted). See Satire, Irony, and Sarcasm.

Satire, Irony, and Sarcasm: Chap. XI. (Modes of ridicule of combined risible and moral inferiorities):

    Satire: (Presents no phases of circumstantial novelty): 249-51.

    Irony: Used in sense of attempted enlightenment, by inference from obvious exaggeration of error. (Presents in each case phase of circumstantial novelty No. 2 belonging to group No. 9, Chap. VI., Pt. III.): 251-5.

    Sarcasm: (Presents phase of circumstantial novelty or not according to occasion): 255-61.

Similes beyond the limits of substantially rational comparison: (*Phases of Circumstantial Novelty No. 2*). Chap. VI., Pt. III.

# INDEX.

Similes within the limits of substantially rational comparison: (Due to ingenuity of 1st species): 8; 48.

Standards to which intrinsic inferiorities are referable:    Chaps. III., IX., and X.

Synopsis of Theory: 7-9.

Verbal quibbles: (*Phases of Circumstantial Novelty No.* 2):    Chap. VI., Pts. I. and II.; and (general references) Chap. V.

    1st Class: Illustrated, 75-81.

    Generic imperfections attending these: 73-4.

    Event of occasion provided sometimes in the ordinary course of things, sometimes by ingenuity of 1st species: 74.

    2nd Class: (Inverted quibbles), 72-3. Illustrated in special category with other jokes by inversion: 143-50.

Wit:

    Term employed in book to designate sub-species of species 3 of Ingenuity: See Ingenuity.

    Senses in which the word is ordinarily used;

        As above: See Ingenuity.

        Mother wit, etc.: 48; 262.

        Ingenuity in general of various kinds: Chaps. V. and VI.

    Bad and indifferent wit: 221.